PRESSBOX ★ LEGENDS

— PRESENTS —

THE STADIUM

• 1 9 2 3 – 2 0 0 8 •

THE STADIUM:

Published in the United States of America
by Word Smith Media Ventures, LLC
3600 Clipper Mill Road, Suite 155
Baltimore, MD 21211

ISBN 978-0-9791975-6-7

Cover and layout design and art direction by Brad Meerholz. Graphic design and layout by Kimberly Shilling. Special Projects editor, Jennifer Nelson. Printed by Whitmore Group.

Stan Charles, Larry Harris, Kevin Heitz, Staci Wolfson, John Coulson, Matt Florio, Mark Luterman, Julie Sawyer, Ashley Campbell, Derek Liberman, Mollie Ann Bracigliano, Howe Burch, Ted Burns, Rich Hollander, Steve Marcus, Marvin Milstein, David Sandora and Ray Schulte.

Jerry Driendl/Getty Images: Cover. Rich Pilling/MLB Photos/Getty Images: Cover inset, 67. MLB Photos/Getty Images: 7. National Baseball Hall of Fame Library/MLB Photos/Getty Images: 8, 29, 69. Diamond Images/Getty Images: 11, 53, 58. Mark Rucker/Transcendental Graphics/Getty Images: 13, 72. Nat Fein/Hulton Archive/Getty Images: 14. Focus on Sport/Getty Images: 19, 55. Louis Requena/MLB Photos/Getty Images: 21. Al Bello/Getty Images: 23, 34. Arnold Newman/Getty Images: 25. Bruce Bennett Studios/Getty Images: 27, 71. Herb Scharfman/Sports Imagery/Getty Images: 33. Robert Riger/Getty Images: 37, 39. Hulton Archive/Getty Images: 41. Dirck Halstead/Time & Life Pictures/Getty Images: 43. Olen Collection/Diamond Images/Getty Images: 47, 49. Ronald C. Modra/Sports Imagery/Getty Images: 56. Matt Campbell/AFP/Getty Images: 61. Ezra Shaw/Getty Images: 63. Mitch Stringer/PressBox: Back cover background.

PRESSBOX ★ LEGENDS

PRESENTS

• THE STADIUM •

1923 - 2008

TABLE OF CONTENTS ★

THE HOUSE THAT RUTH BUILT 4
THOM LOVERRO

TOP 10 YANKEES MOMENTS 10
JOHN DELCOS

WORLD SERIES AT THE STADIUM 16
BILLY ALTMAN

YANKEE SKIPPERS 24
MAURY ALLEN

YANKEE OWNERSHIP: A HISTORY 28
LEE LOWENFISH

TRADITION BY POSITION 32
MAURY ALLEN

LEGACY ON THE GRIDIRON 36
KEN DENLINGER

A BACKDROP TO BOXING 40
BERT RANDOLPH SUGAR

THE PAPAL VISITS 42
MIKE LURIE

OLD-TIMERS' DAYS 46
DAVID GINSBURG

CONSTRUCTION ZONE 50
THOM LOVERRO

MONUMENT PARK LEGENDS 52
CHARLIE VASCELLARO

SOUNDS OF THE STADIUM 57
BILLY ALTMAN

WE'RE ALL NEW YORKERS 60
STEVE JACOBSON

THE YANKEES' NEXT HOME 65
DAVID SANDORA

THE TIMELINE 68
JOHN DELCOS

BY THE NUMBERS 72

hen baseball fans talk about the deal that sent Babe Ruth from the Boston Red Sox to the New York Yankees in 1920, most of the focus is on the "curse" it placed on the Red Sox franchise.

What is often glossed over is the real impact it had on the New York Yankees and the game of baseball – more than just the obvious benefit of having one of the greatest home run hitters in history.

It has become cliché, but Yankee Stadium really was "the House that Ruth Built," because if there was no Ruth, there would be no Taj Mahal-like ballpark completed in the Bronx in 1923, bigger and bolder than anything baseball had ever seen before.

Sr. passed away in 1915. In what has since become a longtime marriage, beer and baseball were tied together when Ruppert and business partner Tillinghast L'Hommedieu Huston bought the run-down New York Highlanders franchise from the team's original owners, Frank Farrell and William S. Devery, for $460,000. Ruppert then began laying the groundwork to turn the Highlanders from a stepchild to the king of baseball in the city.

At the time, the New York Giants ruled baseball in New York. Under the direction of legendary manager John McGraw, the Giants had won five National League pennants after the turn of the century. They played in a ballpark called the Polo Grounds. By this time, it was the fourth version of the Polo Grounds, which had been refurbished after a 1911 fire.

THE HOUSE THAT RUTH BUILT

BY: Thom Loverro

"This stadium was grander and taller and bigger than anything that had come before," said Joe Mock, who is the author of the book "Joe Mock's Ballpark Guide" and operates the Web site www.baseballparks.com. "You have Babe Ruth playing for you, you want it to be bigger and better.

"They felt they had the biggest and the best team, which they did. It changed the landscape of the game with the large crowds they drew there."

Ruth's presence was behind most of the circumstances that led to the construction of Yankee Stadium. But it was another larger-than-life figure that put the club in a position to build a new ballpark in the Bronx – the colorful Tammany Hall politician and owner of the Yankees, Jacob Ruppert.

Ruppert was born in New York in 1867, the son of a wealthy brewer, Jacob Ruppert Sr. The younger Ruppert went on to become a colonel in the National Guard and then carved out a political career himself, elected to Congress in 1898. He served four terms before stepping back into the business world shortly after armed with strong political contacts and even stronger ambitions.

He inherited his father's brewing company when Ruppert

While the Polo Grounds was being rebuilt, the Giants paid rent to play in the Highlanders' home at the time – Hilltop Park. Once the Giants' home was finished in 1912, the Highlanders went from landlords to tenants, playing their home games at the Polo Grounds.

That same year, they changed their name to the New York Yankees.

Ruppert purchased the Yankees and began rebuilding the franchise, hiring Miller Huggins as manager in 1918 and after the 1919 season made the transaction with the Red Sox that changed New York and baseball forever, acquiring a young pitcher-slugger named George Herman Ruth from the Red Sox for $125,000.

Ruth was an outstanding pitcher and hitter in Boston, but the dead ball era was coming to an end, and the Yankees saw the value of the attraction of the home run and used Ruth mostly as a position player. He responded by hitting 54 home runs in 1920, and New York baseball fans responded by filling up the Polo Grounds. In Ruth's first year in 1920, the Yankees drew 1.3 million fans, outdrawing the Giants. The second year, the Yankees were in the World Series playing the

— THE HOUSE THAT RUTH BUILT —

Giants. The Yankees lost the battle of the series, but they were winning the war of baseball in New York.

"There was a time when the Giants were more popular than the Yankees, but then Babe Ruth came along, and the Yankees started becoming more popular than the Giants," Mock said. "The Giants didn't appreciate that, and it caused friction between the two clubs."

So Giants owner Charles Stoneham wanted the tenant to leave to put some distance between the two clubs. The squeeze play blew up in his face.

"The expectation was that they would go out to Long Island or somewhere else," said Neil Sullivan, author of "The Diamond in the Bronx" and a professor at Baruch College. "There was no reason to believe they would go right across the Harlem River."

But they did. They went right across the river, in clear view of their rivals.

"Ruppert had information about the development of the Bronx, which was well underway by the 1920s," Sullivan said. "You had subway lines going out there. The Bronx Terminal Market hadn't been built yet, but it was proposed, and that would have meant a lot of working people who would be finished with work and then have time to go to a ballgame later in the afternoon. He knew about the Bronx Terminal Market coming, and he was able to acquire the land there for the stadium."

Ruppert purchased 10 acres of land at the corner of Eighth Avenue and 155th Street. They hired the foremost ballpark architects at the time, Osborne Engineering out of Cleveland, and 11 months later, April 18, 1923, with John Philip Sousa on hand to perform as they raised the 1922 Yankees' American League pennant, they opened a $2.5 million facility that was unlike anything America had seen before.

Reports show that more than 74,200 fans came for that historic event with a crowd standing outside that didn't get in. The ones that did saw what they came for – a Ruth three-run home run for a 4-1 New York victory.

It was a ballpark for the 1920s, the golden age of sports.

"Every stadium that gets built is a reaction to what was built before," Mock said. "There had been concrete and steel stadiums built around since 1910, but nothing on a scale like this. It was unrivaled at the time. The Yankees wanted the biggest and the best."

A baseball palace, Yankee Stadium had a distinctive look, painted in blue and white with a white frieze that curved around the top of the ballpark with vertical white columns and an arch on the bottom. It was the first three-tiered sports complex in the United States. It was also supposed to be used for track and field with a running track that served as the warning track. The bleachers in left and right field were at right angles to each other and to the stands behind third base to allow for a football layout as well as track and field viewing.

And it was built for Ruth with a 295-foot short porch down the right field line for the left-handed slugger, as well as 429 feet in right-center. But center field was known as "Death Valley" because home runs often died there, the deepest part 490 feet from home plate.

Fans flocked to see Ruth and the mighty Yankees like never before.

"Ballparks back in 1923 held 23,000, maybe 25,000, and all of a sudden they open Yankee Stadium, and in 1923 it had a huge number of seats," said Philip Lowry, author of "Green Cathedrals." "It is very complicated to figure out exactly. The majority of the seats were open bleacher seats without a back. So how to figure out how many seats there are? You just figure out how wide human beings were then, and you guess. Gradually, it changed. They started putting more chairs in, and as that continued from 1923 onward, you started to get figures from Yankee Stadium that were roughly accurate as to how many people could be seated.

"But the number of people that would attend a game at Yankee Stadium in the 1920s would include standing room only and people standing in the aisles, because the fire department didn't really care about that in the 1920s. In my book, the original number is 58,000. That is the first reference in the *New York Times* of the capacity of the stadium. Three years later, they said it was 62,000."

"THIS STADIUM WAS GRANDER AND TALLER AND BIGGER THAN ANYTHING THAT HAD COME BEFORE."

— JOE MOCK —

— THE HOUSE THAT RUTH BUILT —

The following year, the capacity was listed at an astounding 82,000. That was the year of the 1927 Yankees, considered by many the greatest team in history. Ruth made baseball history by slugging 60 home runs, a record that stood for 34 years until another Yankee, Roger Maris, hit 61. The ballpark was living up to the nickname sportswriter Fred Lieb gave it upon its opening, "the House that Ruth Built."

"The Yankees filled it because of Babe Ruth," Lowry said. "The game was changing because of Babe Ruth. He became the vehicle by which the game became more popular. This stadium is a personification of Babe Ruth because it is uniquely extremely short down the foul lines, which enabled Ruth to hit a lot of his home runs, and it is twice as big as any other park, and the Yankees are routinely drawing 75,000 to 80,000 people to the ballpark, standing in the aisles, standing all over the place. Baseball had never seen attendance figures like that. It was unbelievable growth in the game."

In the history of the game, there have only been 20 crowds over 80,000, and most of them were at Yankee Stadium. At the Bronx ballpark, the Yankees drew 82,437 paid May 30, 1940. On May 30, 1938, there were 81,841 paid and 84,042 total. And Sept. 9, 1928, the year after Ruth had hit 60 home runs, Yankee Stadium had the largest crowd ever – 81,622 paid and 85,265 total.

"Yankee Stadium exploded the sport of baseball because it was so big, and there were so many people going to the games," Lowry said.

It may have saved the game, coming on the heels of the 1919 Black Sox gambling scandal that nearly destroyed Major League Baseball.

After 13 seasons, there would be some changes. The wooden bleachers were replaced with concrete bleachers, bringing the center field fence in closer, but it was still a deep shot to get out. The second and third decks were extended to right-center. And changes continued, as the outfield bench seats were replaced with chairs throughout the 1930s and 1940s.

The capacity would change as well, though the large crowds often exceeded capacity, allowing for standing room only crowds.

Whatever the crowd numbered, it was nearly always more than at any other stadium. And while it was a magnificent ballpark, fans didn't come just to admire the architecture. They kept coming because the Yankees kept winning, with star players that became American icons, like Ruth and his counterpart at first base, Lou Gehrig.

With Ruth and/or Gehrig on the Yankees' roster from 1920 to 1939, the World Series took place at Yankee Stadium 11 times, with the Yankees winning eight titles. Ruth was released after the 1934 season. Gehrig remained the "Iron Man" and played in 2,130 consecutive games until his career was cut short by amyotrophic lateral sclerosis (ALS), now known as Lou Gehrig's Disease.

The Yankees declared July 4, 1939 "Lou Gehrig Appreciation Day" at the stadium, and the world saw one of the most historic and touching events in the history of baseball, Gehrig's goodbye speech. Between games of a doubleheader against the Washington Senators, he stood before the crowd of more than 62,000 fans who cheered and cried for their hero. New York Mayor Fiorello LaGuardia called Gehrig "the greatest prototype of good sportsmanship and citizenship." His No. 4 was retired that day, the first one in Yankees history, and Gehrig, though weakened by his illness, had strength in his words that still hold up today.

"Fans, for the past two weeks you have been reading about the bad break I got," he said. "Yet today, I consider myself the luckiest man on the face of this earth. I have been in ballparks for 17 years and have never received anything but kindness and encouragement from you fans." It capped one of the most poignant moments ever seen in sports, taking place on one of the greatest stages ever built for sports.

It was the end of an era but not the end of the Yankees dynasty, and the crowds continued to come to the historic ballpark. Another icon, Joe DiMaggio, also captured the hearts of Yankees fans. The "Yankee Clipper" made his debut in 1936 and became one of the greatest all-around

[THE FANS] KEPT COMING BECAUSE THE YANKEES KEPT WINNING.

— THE HOUSE THAT RUTH BUILT —

★

YANKEE STADIUM OPENED ITS DOORS ON APRIL 18, 1923.

players the game had ever seen.

In 1941, Yankees fans witnessed perhaps the greatest sports record ever set. DiMaggio hit in 56 straight games from May 15 to July 16. During his career from 1936 to 1951, Yankee Stadium hosted 11 World Series, and the Yankees won 10 of them. Unlike Ruth, DiMaggio did not benefit from his home park. He hit 361 career home runs, and probably lost many more in the deep left and left-center field sections of the ballpark. But he became an American icon playing in New York.

During the DiMaggio era at Yankee Stadium, ownership of the team changed hands. In 1945, Dan Topping, developer Del Webb and former Brooklyn Dodgers owner Larry MacPhail purchased the Yankees from Ruppert's estate for $2.8 million.

The crowds and the dynasty continued in 1951 with the arrival of another soon-to-be Yankees legend named Mickey Mantle. His good looks and talent helped sustain the Yankees dynasty both on and off the field as he won three Most Valuable Player awards and the Triple Crown in 1956. He also engaged in a historic home run duel with teammate Maris in 1961 when Maris broke Ruth's record of 60 home runs. Mantle fell short that year because of

injuries, hitting 54 home runs, while Maris hit his 61st on the last day of the season at Yankee Stadium. With Mantle on the squad from 1951 to 1968, the Yankees played in 12 World Series and won seven.

The stadium was still the biggest baseball stage in America and sometimes beyond, hosting football's New York Giants for 17 years as well as soccer games, championship fights, concerts, religious services conducted by two popes and the Rev. Billy Graham, and a celebration of Nelson Mandela's 1989 visit to the United States.

For players making their debut as a Yankee, sometimes the scene was overwhelming. It was when catcher Johnny Blanchard first entered the ballpark in 1955.

"It was a full house, a doubleheader against the Red Sox," Blanchard said. "I had never seen that many people before. I didn't think there were that many people in the world. It was frightening when you walk in the stadium the first time and see that. I will never forget it.

"Charlie Silvera was coaching, and I was in the bullpen, and he picked up the phone as it rang and then said, 'Hey, Blanch, they want you to pinch hit.' I couldn't even stand up. I said, 'Call them back. I can't run from the bullpen to home plate.' Then everyone broke up.

— THE HOUSE THAT RUTH BUILT —

They knew he was pulling my leg. I had butterflies coming out of my eyeballs. It is a historic place, and you can almost feel Babe Ruth, Lou Gehrig, Joe DiMaggio and all of those players with you there."

However, the streak of stars was about to hit a dry spell with Mantle's retirement, and the franchise was falling on hard times, suffering five losing seasons from 1965 to 1973. This fall coincided with a disastrous change of ownership. In 1964, Columbia Broadcasting System bought 80 percent of the club for $11.2 million and later purchased the remaining 20 percent.

The ballpark had seen its better days, falling into disrepair. The combination of losing along with the condition of the ballpark and the deterioration of the South Bronx resulted in empty seats, a stunning development. In 1972, the Yankees fell below 1 million fans for the first time in nearly 20 years. One year later, the fortunes of the team changed, and so did the future of Yankee Stadium. George Steinbrenner III, a shipbuilder from Cleveland, purchased the Yankees from CBS for $10 million.

Steinbrenner brought a football mentality to baseball that he developed as a graduate assistant to legendary Ohio State football coach Woody Hayes. He was forceful and controversial, but he had a vision of what the Yankees were and what they should be – winning star players. He took full advantage of the birth of free agency by spending whatever it took to sign stars Catfish Hunter and Reggie Jackson. From 1976 to 1981, Yankee Stadium hosted four World Series with the Bronx Bombers winning two of them.

At the same time Steinbrenner took over the team,

New York Mayor John Lindsay stepped in and announced the city would buy Yankee Stadium for $24 million. The stadium was closed for the 1974 and 1975 seasons, and $160 million was spent to refurbish the ballpark, modernizing it but also making it different than "the House that Ruth Built."

The Yankees played at Shea Stadium, sharing the New York Mets' home field, for those two seasons. The dimensions on the field at Yankee Stadium were reduced, particularly the deep center field, and capacity was now at 57,545. The changes appeared well received by fans, as attendance regularly topped 2 million a year, even during some tumultuous times and a postseason drought from 1981 to 1995.

But starting in 1996, under new manager Joe Torre and a team led by homegrown stars Derek Jeter and Bernie Williams, Yankee Stadium became the home of the World Series again, as the stadium hosted the Fall Classic six of the next eight seasons, with four Yankees teams crowned World Champions. And yearly attendance records have been set since that 1996 run began, even though the Yankees have not been to the World Series since 2003. In 1998, they went over 3 million for the first time, drawing 3.2 million, and in 2005, more than 4 million fans made the pilgrimage to Yankee Stadium.

Just as it was when it opened in 1923, Yankee Stadium, even in its final year of existence before the new version opens next door, remains the most important stadium in baseball. ☐

★

YANKEE STADIUM'S SHORT RIGHT FIELD LINE WAS
A PERFECT FIT FOR SLUGGER BABE RUTH.

THOM LOVERRO IS A COLUMNIST FOR THE WASHINGTON TIMES AND HAS PUBLISHED SEVERAL BOOKS, INCLUDING "HOME OF THE GAME: THE STORY OF CAMDEN YARDS."

THE YANKEES
YEAR BY YEAR RECORDS

YEAR	W	L	PCT.	YEAR	W	L	PCT.	YEAR	W	L	PCT.
2008				1972	79	76	.510	1936	102	51	.667
2007	94	68	.580	1971	82	80	.506	1935	89	60	.597
2006	97	65	.599	1970	93	69	.574	1934	94	60	.610
2005	95	67	.586	1969	80	81	.497	1933	91	59	.607
2004	101	61	.623	1968	83	79	.512	1932	107	47	.695
2003	101	61	.623	1967	72	90	.444	1931	94	59	.614
2002	103	58	.640	1966	70	89	.440	1930	86	68	.558
2001	95	65	.594	1965	77	85	.475	1929	88	66	.571
2000	87	74	.540	1964	99	63	.611	1928	101	53	.656
1999	98	64	.605	1963	104	57	.646	1927	110	44	.714
1998	114	48	.704	1962	96	66	.593	1926	91	63	.591
1997	96	66	.593	1961	109	53	.673	1925	69	85	.448
1996	92	70	.568	1960	97	57	.630	1924	89	63	.586
1995	79	65	.549	1959	79	75	.513	1923	98	54	.645
1994	70	43	.619	1958	92	62	.597	1922 *	94	60	.610
1993	88	74	.543	1957	98	56	.636	1921 *	98	55	.641
1992	76	86	.469	1956	97	57	.630	1920 *	95	59	.617
1991	71	91	.438	1955	96	58	.623	1919 *	80	59	.576
1990	67	95	.414	1954	103	51	.669	1918 *	60	63	.488
1989	74	87	.460	1953	99	52	.656	1917 *	71	82	.464
1988	85	76	.528	1952	95	59	.617	1916 *	80	74	.519
1987	89	73	.549	1951	98	56	.636	1915 *	69	83	.454
1986	90	72	.556	1950	98	56	.636	1914 *	70	84	.455
1985	97	64	.602	1949	97	57	.630	1913 *	57	94	.377
1984	87	75	.537	1948	94	60	.610	1912 *	50	102	.329
1983	91	71	.562	1947	97	57	.630	1911 *	76	76	.500
1982	79	83	.488	1946	87	67	.565	1910 *	88	63	.583
1981	59	48	.551	1945	81	71	.533	1909 *	74	77	.490
1980	103	59	.636	1944	83	71	.539	1908 *	51	103	.331
1979	89	71	.556	1943	98	56	.636	1907 *	70	78	.473
1978	100	63	.613	1942	103	51	.669	1906 *	90	61	.596
1977	100	62	.617	1941	101	53	.656	1905 *	71	78	.477
1976	97	62	.610	1940	88	66	.571	1904 *	92	59	.609
1975 *	83	77	.519	1939	106	45	.702	1903 *	72	62	.537
1974 *	89	73	.549	1938	99	53	.651				
1973	80	82	.494	1937	102	52	.662				

Note: The team played as the New York Highlanders from 1903 to 1912.

* Indicates seasons NOT at Yankee Stadium.

Red denotes years the Yankees won the World Series.

TOP 10 YANKEES MOMENTS

BY: John Delcos

Selecting the top 10 moments at Yankee Stadium is a nearly impossible task – the kind that keeps sports radio humming through the late-night hours. Nevertheless, here are 10 unforgettable Yankees occasions that have taken place through the years, from one to 10.

★

OCT. 8, 1956
A MOMENT OF PERFECTION

It is one of the most enduring images in sports, Yankees catcher Yogi Berra jumping into the arms of pitcher Don Larsen after the only perfect game in World Series history to beat the Brooklyn Dodgers, 2-0, in Game 5. With today's emphasis on bullpens, it is doubtful there will be another.

Larsen's career was a study in mediocrity except for the afternoon when the Dodgers flailed helplessly, the game ending with a checked-swing strikeout of Dale Mitchell. Ripped in Game 2, Larsen prepared for history with a night on the town with a writer, missing curfew by 10 minutes.

Mickey Mantle staked Larsen to a 1-0 lead in the fourth with a home run and later saved the no-hitter when he raced into the left-center gap to rob Gil Hodges with a back-handed catch.

"Mantle made a beautiful catch," Larsen said. "That ball probably would have been a home run in most parks, but Yankee Stadium at that time was pretty big in left-center. Mantle could run like a deer, caught that ball, and I had another sigh of relief."

Larsen pitched three more seasons with the Yankees and retired after a 14-year career with an 81-91 record.

"I think about it every day," he said. "Sometimes, it's hard to believe it ever happened. I'm glad it did because everybody thinks about that and forgets all the mistakes I made in my career."

★

JULY 4, 1939
THE LUCKIEST MAN

Lou Gehrig knew he was dying the day he told the crowd he considered himself the "luckiest man on the face of this earth" in one of baseball's most poignant moments. The strength of the "Iron Horse" was getting sapped by amyotrophic lateral sclerosis (ALS) – the disease that would eventually bear his name – to the point where it forced him to sit out the May 2 game in Detroit, snapping his consecutive games streak of 2,130 games.

Manager Joe McCarthy left the decision up to Gehrig, who held firm. Three times that afternoon, Gehrig's replacement, Babe Dahlgren, pleaded with him to play to preserve the streak.

"I appreciate it, Babe," Gehrig said. "But I'm done."

Not quite though. Gehrig, who never struck the same emotional chord with the fans as Babe Ruth, wanted to back down on his speech but was prodded by more than 62,000 who chanted his name.

"Fans, for the past two weeks you have been reading about a bad break I got," Gehrig began in what would be called baseball's Gettysburg Address. "Yet today, I consider myself the luckiest man on the face of this earth. I have been in ballparks for 17 years and have never received anything but kindness and encouragement from you fans. Look at these grand men. Which of you wouldn't consider it the highlight of his career just to associate with them for even one day? Sure, I'm lucky."

After the speech, in another enduring image, Ruth embraced Gehrig in the first contact between the feuding former teammates in five years. Gehrig died June 2, 1941.

— TOP 10 YANKEES MOMENTS —

JUNE 13, 1948
BABE SAYS GOODBYE

Ruth not only personified baseball, but to many he was the face of America. It is said that Japanese soldiers in the Pacific Theater cursed his name in hopes of provoking United States Marines to expose their positions. How do you say farewell to a legend?

The Yankees, knowing Ruth was dying, had chosen the day to mark the 25th year of Yankee Stadium and opted to honor baseball's most famous player by retiring his No. 3. Ruth's cherub grin had turned taut, his eyes sunken when he wore his Yankees uniform for the last time. The telephone pole of a bat he once used to terrorize pitchers he now leaned on for support.

Nat Fein's photo taken from behind turned out to be one of the most memorable sports photographs in history. Ruth stood at the plate as the crowd engulfed him.

"He walked out into that cauldron of sound he must have known better than any other man," wrote W.C. Heinz.

★

DON LARSEN CELEBRATES WITH YOGI BERRA
AFTER THE FINAL PITCH OF HIS PERFECT GAME
IN THE 1956 WORLD SERIES.

Ruth broke through the cheers to speak to the crowd with a gravelly voice not much louder than a whisper made so by cancer. He would return to "the House that Ruth Built" two months later, as a crowd of more than 100,000 stretched around the cavernous stadium waiting for hours for a chance to say goodbye as he lay in his casket.

★

SEPT. 30, 1927
BABE HITS 60

It was Ruth who saved baseball after the 1919 Black Sox scandal as he captivated the public with his gregarious personality, his flair for the dramatic and his large appetites for hot dogs and women. But above all else, his tremendous power captivated fans.

"Babe Ruth is still relevant the way George Washington is still relevant," said Leigh Montville, author of "The Big Bam: The Life and Times of Babe Ruth." "Babe Ruth is an icon. He's a lion from the past. He kind of invented the home run. He forged the way for everything that has happened since in baseball. Before him, a home run was basically an accident, but he comes along with an uppercut swing and changes everything. He's responsible for all the stuff that followed."

One of the amazing things about Ruth's 60th homer, hit off Washington's Tom Zachary, is it equaled the combined total hit by National League co-leaders Cy Williams of Philadelphia and Hack Wilson of Chicago, each with 30. More mind-boggling is that no American League team and only three NL teams hit as many as 60 that season.

Ruth, of course, held the record of 59 set in 1921. He needed to hit eight with 14 games remaining to break his own record, which he did on the next-to-last game of the season. After the game, Ruth is said to have yelled in the clubhouse, "Sixty homers, let's see somebody match that."

★

OCT. 1, 1961
ROGER PASSES BABE

Roger Maris joined the Yankees in 1960 and hit 39 home runs to go along with his solid play in right field. Casey Stengel called him "the best man I ever got in a deal," but

— TOP 10 YANKEES MOMENTS —

BABE RUTH RECEIVED A STANDING OVATION FROM THE FANS AS HIS NUMBER WAS RETIRED ON JUNE 13, 1948.

Aug. 18 after Brett's homer. The Yankees went into a tailspin, losing six of seven games.

"Mentally, it really hurt us," Martin said. "We felt we had a game taken away from us because of a play that was illegal. It was hard for our guys to accept." AL president Lee MacPhail ruled in favor of the Royals, saying Brett hadn't done anything deceptive.

"In the end it counted, so while I may have been angry, I can't be known as a cheater because the league made it count," Brett said.

★
OCT. 14, 1976:
CHAMBLISS' HOMER
WINS THE ALCS

Talk softly, but carry a big bat. That was Chambliss. He had driven in three runs with a two-run homer for a 5-3 victory in Game 3 of the ALCS against Kansas City, but he carved his place in Yankees lore in Game 5.

The Yankees took a 6-3 lead into the eighth, but Brett tied the game with a three-run homer. The Yankee Stadium crowd had turned ugly, and fans littered the field with firecrackers, toilet tissue and other debris. Chambliss didn't appreciate the wait.

"I was a little anxious," he said. "It was cold too. That was a trying time."

Chambliss stepped in against Royals reliever Mark Littell, who won eight games and saved 16. He was thinking Littell would try to get ahead early in the count.

"I knew Littell was going to throw a fastball," said Chambliss, who turned on the pitch and lined it on a rope to right, where Hal McRae had no chance. Chambliss also had no chance of making it around the bases. Fans stormed the field, taking gloves, hats and even second base.

"By the time Chris got to third base, all hope of reaching the plate was gone," Munson said. "He never did make it."

Well, not right away. Long after the crowd had left, Chambliss walked out of the Yankees' dugout and touched the plate. □

JOHN DELCOS COVERED THE NEW YORK YANKEES FROM 1998 TO 2005 FOR GANNETT NEWSPAPERS (THE JOURNAL NEWS) IN WESTCHESTER, N.Y. HE CURRENTLY COVERS THE NEW YORK METS AND MAJOR LEAGUE BASEBALL.

TAKE ME OUT TO THE BALL GAME. TAKE ME OUT TO THE CROWD. BUY ME SOME PEANUTS AND CRACKER JACK,® AND SOME DONUTS, GOURMET COFFEE, A PACK OF GUM, AND A CAR WASH, TWO BOTTLES OF SODA AND A BAG OF TORTILLA CHIPS AND A COLD ICE CREAM AND

EXXON **Mobil** Life. On the Run

Since its opening in 1923, Yankee Stadium has hosted games in 37 of 84 World Series. Through 2007, of the Yankees' 26 championships, nine were clinched at home; seven times, it was their opponents who celebrated in New York.

★
1923: YANKEES 4, GIANTS 2

After playing at the New York Giants' Polo Grounds in Manhattan for the previous 10 years, the opening of the new ballpark in the Bronx proved to be the third-time charm for the Yankees in the World Series. Beaten in both the 1921 and '22 World Series by their old Giants landlords, the '23 Yankees captured their first world championship with a 4-2 series win over their crosstown

winning run, Ruth made an ill-advised attempt at stealing second. He was thrown out to end the game, concluding one of the most memorable Fall Classics ever.

★
1927: YANKEES 4, PIRATES 0

Led by Ruth's record-setting 60 home runs and Lou Gehrig's 174 RBIs, the "Murderers' Row" Yankees of 1927 outscored opponents by nearly 400 runs. The pitching wasn't too shabby either, as Waite Hoyt (22-7) and Herb Pennock (19-8) fronted a staff that led the league in ERA. Arguably the greatest baseball team ever, the '27 Yanks (110-44) proved too much for the National League Pirates, who were swept in four. For all their firepower, the Yankees won the final game at home in the bottom of the ninth on small ball with two walks, a bunt single and

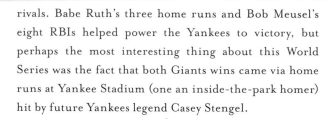

WORLD SERIES AT THE STADIUM

BY: Billy Altman

rivals. Babe Ruth's three home runs and Bob Meusel's eight RBIs helped power the Yankees to victory, but perhaps the most interesting thing about this World Series was the fact that both Giants wins came via home runs at Yankee Stadium (one an inside-the-park homer) hit by future Yankees legend Casey Stengel.

★
1926: CARDINALS 4, YANKEES 3

The Yanks were leading this seesaw series, 3-2, but player/manager Rogers Hornsby's Cardinals took the championship by winning the final two games in New York, largely through the heroics of pitcher Grover Cleveland Alexander. After going the distance in Game 6, Alexander came out of the bullpen the next day in the seventh with the bases loaded and his team clinging to a 3-2 lead. The 39-year-old righty struck out rookie Tony Lazzeri to end the threat, and the score stayed that way until the ninth. With two outs and none on, Alexander faced Ruth, who had slammed a record-setting three home runs in Game 4 and had again homered earlier that day. Ruth walked (his 11th of the series), but with Meusel at the plate representing the

a run-scoring, series-ending wild pitch.

★
1928: YANKEES 4, CARDINALS 0

Manager Miller Huggins' injury-riddled team needed until the next-to-last day of the season to clinch the American League pennant, but the 1928 Yankees picked right up where the '27 squad left off, notching their second straight World Series sweep. This time, the victims were the Cardinals, who led for just one half-inning during the four games. Unlike in 1926, the St. Louis pitchers, even Alexander, were helpless against the one-two punch of Ruth and Gehrig. Going 10-for-16 for an astonishing .625 batting average, Ruth repeated his three-homers-in-one-game feat in the Game 4 clincher in St. Louis. With just 11 official at-bats, Gehrig clubbed four home runs and six hits for nine RBIs.

★
1932: YANKEES 4, CUBS 0

While absent from the World Series for several years, the '32 Yankees, now managed by Joe McCarthy,

— WORLD SERIES AT THE STADIUM —

Yankees' wins i
pitching from R.
winning Game (
staged a late-inn
a grounder off h
lefty later claim
that contest, 3-2
with a 4-2 victc
up grab of Jack
might have turr
for the Dodger:

★

1953: YAN
DODGE

After goi
(0-for-21)
the entire 1
Series, the I
Hodges batted
redeeming .3(
in the 1953 V
Unfortunately
teams knotted
apiece, the us
Hodges mad
fielding erro:
that set the sta
slam by y(
Mantle, as N
11-7. The seri
to the Bronx
where the E
3-1 lead in t
Carl Furillo
still won the
Martin, whc
24, with twc
York an unp
feat still unp

195!

After los
Series meet
rights when
While Ster

needed only the minimum four games to wrap up another championship. Emerging aces Red Ruffing and Lefty Gomez each went all the way in Games 1 and 2 in New York, while old dependables George Pipgras and Pennock combined for a 7-5 Game 3 victory in Chicago. That fabled contest featured two homers each from Gehrig and Ruth, whose finger-pointing gesture toward the outfield before a mammoth clout off Charlie Root became part of baseball lore. As Ruth made his final World Series appearance, Gehrig hit .529. Not far behind was young Bill Dickey, who batted .438 and helped win Game 4 with three hits.

★

1936: YANKEES 4, GIANTS 2

Comparable offensively to their 1927 predecessors, the '36 Yankees boasted a lineup featuring five players with more than 100 RBIs, none more talked about than 21-year-old rookie Joe DiMaggio. Giants ace Carl "King" Hubbell stymied DiMaggio and his mates in Game 1, ending the Yankees' streak of 12 consecutive World Series wins. After that, though, the Bronx bats took over, and the Yanks scored 18 runs in Game 2 and 13 in the Game 6 finale at the Polo Grounds. Contributions came from veterans Lazerri (a grand slam, seven RBIs) and Gehrig (two home runs, seven RBIs).

★

1937: YANKEES 4, GIANTS 1

McCarthy's Yankees and Bill Terry's Giants squared off for back-to-back New York World Series, and once again the Bombers prevailed. The Yanks took the first two contests at home by identical 8-1 scores, with complete game victories from Gomez and then Ruffing, who chipped in at the plate with two hits and three RBIs. After winning Game 3, the Yankees seemed poised for a sweep, but McCarthy gave the Game 4 start to rotation low man Bump Hadley, whom the Giants rocked for five runs in 1.1 innings en route to a 7-3 win. The next day, Gomez fired a second gem, knocking in the go-ahead run as the Yanks clinched, 4-2.

★

1938: YANKEES 4, CUBS 0

Balanced hitting and stingy pitching helped the Yankees become the first team ever to capture three straight World Series crowns as they swept the overmatched Cubs. Opening in Chicago, New York took

Game 1 behind Ruffing, whose complete-game effort was supported by Dickey's four-hit performance. Sore-armed Dizzy Dean gamely held the Yanks in check for most of Game 2, but he lost after yielding late-inning two-run homers to Frank Crosetti and DiMaggio. Moving to New York, the hero of Game 3 was rookie Joe Gordon, who homered and drove in three runs. Crosetti again led the way in the Game 4 series-ending 8-3 victory at home with a double, triple and four RBIs.

★

1939: YANKEES 4, REDS 0

Cementing dynasty status, the Yankees won a fourth consecutive championship in 1939 via another sweep. With Gehrig's career ended by illness, DiMaggio became the team leader. But the biggest star of this World Series was rookie Charlie Keller. "King Kong" was a one-man wrecking crew, both in the box and on the bases. He tripled and scored the winning run in the bottom of the ninth of Game 1, hit two two-run homers in Game 3 and belted another round-tripper in Game 4. In that final extra-inning affair in Cincinnati, Keller's home plate crash into Ernie Lombardi left the Reds catcher so dazed he couldn't find the ball as DiMaggio also scored, ensuring the victory. "Lombardi's Snooze" remains a World Series legend.

★

1941: YANKEES 4, DODGERS 1

In an already historical season marked by DiMaggio's 56-game hitting streak, the '41 Bombers played their first World Series against their Brooklyn neighbors, managed by ex-Yankee Leo Durocher. The Dodgers were one out away from tying the series at two at home in Game 4 when Hugh Casey threw strike three past a swinging Tommy Henrich. But the ball bounced off catcher Mickey Owen's glove and Henrich reached first safely. The most famous (or infamous) passed ball in World Series history, Owen's miscue opened the floodgates for the Yankees, who exploded for four unearned runs to win the game, riding the momentum to a World Series win at Ebbets Field the next day.

★

1942: CARDINALS 4, YANKEES 1

The '42 Yankees were favored to beat the Cardinals, who had won a grueling pennant race on the final day of the season, and the World Series opener began with New York

taking a 7·
mounted
the bases
Stan Mus
Musial re
The serie
denied. T
finale de
off Ruff
marked t

194

Again
McCart
favor by
While st
were ser
fielded
who all
wins. C
0 clinc
inning
World

1

A tr
host o
Thoug
Game
throw
when
on a
Field
Game
sensa
run h
The
game
Relia

H
a ma
a dis

• THE STADIUM •

— WORLD SERIES AT THE STADIUM —

★
1978: YANKEES 4, DODGERS 2

This rematch of the 1977 World Series ended with the same result, as the Yankees (managed by Bob Lemon, who had taken over at midseason for the fired Martin) again bested Tommy Lasorda's crew in six. This time it was defense that took center stage, as third baseman Graig Nettles helped New York climb back from an 0-2 hole with several spectacular plays in the Game 3 momentum-changing 5-1 win at Yankee Stadium. After that, the Yankees rolled, winning the next three and clinching with a 7-2 Game 6 victory in Los Angeles. Series MVP honors went to Bucky Dent, who hit safely in all six games. But the unsung hero was Brian Doyle, who hit .438 (7-for-16) and played flawless second base filling in for the injured Willie Randolph.

★
1981: DODGERS 4, YANKEES 2

The Yankees and Dodgers squared off for the third time in five years, and this time Los Angeles prevailed. New York won the first two games at home behind Ron Guidry and Tommy John, but things changed when the teams headed to California. Rookie phenom Fernando Valenzuela pitched a complete game as Los Angeles took Game 3, sloppy Yankees fielding helped the Dodgers win Game 4, and Jerry Reuss out-dueled Guidry, 2-1, in Game 5. Back in the Bronx for Game 6, the Dodgers finished off the reeling Yankees in a 9-2 rout, as reliever George Frazier was tagged with his third loss of the series, and Dave Winfield, playing in his lone World Series as a Yankee, batted .045 (1-for-22).

★
1996: YANKEES 4, BRAVES 2

Under new manager Joe Torre, the '96 Yankees secured a World Series berth after a 15-year drought. The Braves buried the Bombers in the Bronx in Game 1, 12-1, as 19-year-old Andruw Jones became the youngest player to hit a World Series home run, and Greg Maddux shut out the Yankees in Game 2. The Yanks took Game 3 in Atlanta, but prospects looked dim after the Braves jumped out to a 6-0 lead in Game 4. New York fought back, tying the game on a three-run homer by Jim Leyritz, and the Yankees won, 8-6, in extra innings. With that, the momentum shifted. Andy Pettitte bested John Smoltz, 1-0, and the Yankees came home to clinch in six as Jimmy Key beat Maddux, 3-2.

★
1998: YANKEES 4, PADRES 0

After winning an astounding 114 games in the regular season, the perfectly balanced '98 Yankees made short work of San Diego, taking four straight. Chuck Knoblauch's three-run shot and Tino Martinez's gland slam powered New York to a 9-6 home win in Game 1. Orlando "El Duque" Hernandez baffled the Padres in Game 2 for a 9-3 win. Moving to San Diego, Scott Brosius' second homer of the game, a three-run shot off Padres closer Trevor Hoffman, lifted New York to a 5-4 win. The Yankees then completed the sweep, 3-0, behind Pettitte and another RBI by Brosius, who finished with a .471 batting average and was deservedly named World Series MVP.

★
1999: YANKEES 4, BRAVES 0

New York took back-to-back championships for the first time since 1977-78 with another sweep. Hernandez yielded just one hit and fanned 10 over seven innings as the Yankees bested Maddux in Game 1, 4-1, and David Cone threw seven shutout innings in the 7-2 win in Game 2. Moving to the Bronx, the Yankees were down 5-1 in Game 3 before Chad Curtis, Knoblauch and Martinez all homered off Tom Glavine to tie the contest and send it into extra innings. Curtis ended things with a second homer, giving New York a 6-5 win. Roger Clemens beat Smoltz in Game 4, 4-1, for the clincher, which was closed out by World Series MVP Mariano Rivera, who notched two saves and a win in 4.2 scoreless innings.

★
2000: YANKEES 4, METS 1

The first World Series matchup between the Yankees and Mets was an intense affair, with each game decided by two runs or less. The tone was set in Game 1 at Yankee Stadium, as the Bombers erased a 3-2 Mets lead with a ninth-inning rally and won in 12, 4-3. The 6-5 Yankees victory in Game 2 featured controversy after Clemens threw a broken bat at Mets slugger Mike Piazza, whom Clemens had beaned earlier that year. The series moved to Shea Stadium, where the Mets broke the Yankees' 14-

— WORLD SERIES AT THE STADIUM —

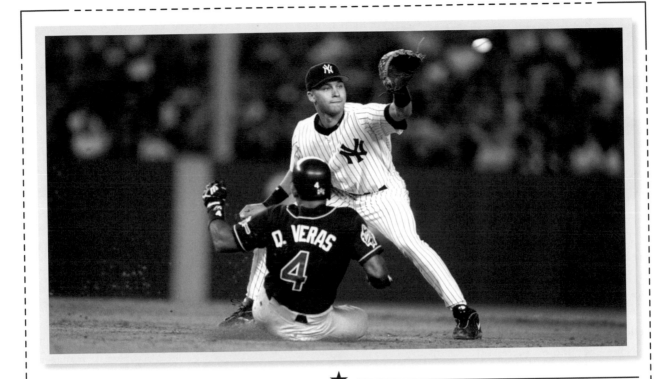

DEREK JETER MAKES A PLAY DURING THE 1998 WORLD SERIES AS THE YANKEES DEFEAT THE PADRES.

★

game World Series winning streak with a 4-2 triumph. However, the Bombers bounced back to take Game 4, 3-2, and wrapped up their third straight championship with a 4-2 victory on a Luis Sojo ninth-inning single off ex-Yankee Al Leiter.

★

2001: DIAMONDBACKS 4, YANKEES 3

The 2001 World Series was a thriller in which each team won all its home games. Curt Schilling and Randy Johnson subdued the Yankees in the first two games in Arizona, but New York swept all three in New York. In Game 4, Martinez slammed a game-tying homer in the bottom of the ninth off closer Byung-Hyun Kim, and Derek Jeter rocked Kim for a game-winning walk-off blast in the 10th. The next night, Kim surrendered another ninth-inning game-tying homer, this time to Brosius, and the Bombers triumphed in extra innings. The Diamondbacks evened the series in Arizona with a 15-2 blowout, setting up a dramatic Game 7. Fittingly, it came down to the bottom of the ninth when Rivera's throwing error led to an Arizona rally that climaxed with

Luis Gonzalez's game-ending single, giving Arizona its first title – and Rivera the first blown save of his World Series career.

★

2003: MARLINS 4, YANKEES 2

Following their dramatic win over Boston in the AL Championship Series, few thought the Yankees would have much trouble with NL wild card Florida. Jack McKeon's young Marlins proved to be more than worthy opponents, however. After falling behind two games to one, Florida overcame a blown save by closer Ugueth Urbina to win Game 4 on an extra-inning homer by Alex Gonzalez off little-used Jeff Weaver. After that, the underdog Marlins couldn't be denied. Brad Penny won his second start against the Yankees in Game 5, and in New York for Game 6, Josh Beckett fired a dazzling five-hitter as the Marlins shut out the Yankees, 2-0, to capture the crown in stunning fashion. ☐

BILLY ALTMAN HAS WRITTEN ABOUT BASEBALL FOR THE NEW YORK TIMES, THE VILLAGE VOICE, NEW YORK MAGAZINE, INSIDE SPORTS AND NUMEROUS OTHER PUBLICATIONS. HE ALSO WORKS AS AN OFFICIAL SCORER FOR MAJOR LEAGUE BASEBALL AT BOTH YANKEE AND SHEA STADIUMS.

— YANKEE SKIPPERS —

sidelined him in September.

"Roger came to me the last week and said he was too tired to play," Houk once said. "I told him to go out there because the fans really wanted him to try. I said if he looked too tired I would pull him out. Then I never looked at him the rest of the game."

Houk turned the managerial chore over to Berra in 1964. He might have sensed that Mantle, Maris, Ford, Elston Howard, Tony Kubek and Bobby Richardson were showing more gray in their hair than snap in their steps.

Berra squeezed out a come-from-behind win, but he lost a bitter seven-game series to Johnny Keane's St. Louis Cardinals. Bob Gibson, pitching on two days of rest, beat the Yankees, 7-5, in the final game despite giving up nine hits and three homers by Mantle, Clete Boyer and the play-me-or-keep-me Yankee, Phil Linz.

When asked after the game why he didn't bring in a relief pitcher for the tired Gibson, Keane replied, "I had a commitment to his heart."

That probably earned Keane a shot at the Yankees' job when Houk, now the general manager of the Yankees under Columbia Broadcasting System ownership, fired Berra.

Keane's team fell to sixth in 1965 and was on its way to a franchise-worst 10th-place finish in 1966 when Houk pulled the plug on the manager and put himself back in uniform and on the Yankees' bench as field boss.

Houk's second tour of duty resulted in a victory drought, with only one finish as high as second in his final eight years as manager.

Bill Virdon was next on the managerial list, but things didn't pick up again around Yankee Stadium until Martin came on board late in 1975. Martin had dreamed of being the Yankees' manager after being sent away as a player

[BILLY] MARTIN HAD DREAMED OF BEING THE YANKEES' MANAGER AFTER BEING SENT AWAY AS A PLAYER ALMOST 20 YEARS EARLIER.

almost 20 years earlier.

Martin led the Yankees to a pennant in 1976 under the new leader, George Steinbrenner, who had purchased the team from CBS in 1973 for a modest $10 million. The new boss spent money freely and foolishly and would settle for nothing less than a World Series title.

He brought in free agents Catfish Hunter and Reggie Jackson in hopes of restoring the team to its exalted role as baseball's leader. With Jackson came turmoil. He fought with Thurman Munson, Martin fought with Steinbrenner, and the rest of the Yankees generally fought with one another. The Yankees won three pennants in a row, two in 1976 and 1977 under Martin and one in 1978 after Martin was replaced by Bob Lemon.

In his second stint with the Yankees, Lemon won another pennant in 1981 but lost out to the Dodgers in the World Series with future Hall of Famer Dave Winfield failing to deliver. He was 1-for-22 in that series. Steinbrenner labeled him "Mr. May" for his October failures in contrast to Jackson, whose five home runs in the 1977 World Series earned him the title of "Mr. October."

The Yankees went 18 years without a title from 1978 to 1996. They paraded managers through the team's office with as much speed as Cool Papa Bell had in the old Negro Leagues, when he was described as a guy who was so fast he could turn out a light in his room and be in bed before it got dark.

Martin had his fifth tour of Steinbrenner duty and was rumored to be ready for No. 6 when he was killed in a car accident on Christmas Day in 1989. Gene Michael, Clyde King, Lou Piniella, Dallas Green, Bucky Dent, even Berra and Stump Merrill (dubbed "Bump Merrill" by Steinbrenner) filled out the lineup cards in those losing years.

Buck Showalter, the tightest drum in town,

— YANKEE SKIPPERS —

took over in 1992, but after he failed against the Seattle Mariners in the 1995 AL Division Series, Steinbrenner started looking around again for a manager who could win it all.

————————— ★ —————————

Torre was born in Brooklyn July 18, 1940. He was a New York Giants fan as a kid, a dangerous claim in the New York City borough of the Dodgers. He began a sparkling playing career with the Milwaukee Braves and played for the St. Louis Cardinals and New York Mets as a catcher, third baseman and first baseman. He batted .297 over 18 seasons, won a batting title and was named the National League Most Valuable Player in 1971.

Torre joined the Mets in 1977 as a player/manager, and his best pitcher, Tom Seaver, was traded away 15 days later. His Mets never finished higher than fifth. He went to the Braves, got close a couple of times in Atlanta, but couldn't make it to the World Series.

He took a half-dozen years off from the field for a broadcasting career and returned as field boss of the Cardinals from 1990 to 1995 without much success.

When Steinbrenner decided to make one of his frequent managerial moves in late 1995, he knew Showalter was the guy he didn't want. But he had no idea about the guy he did want.

"Why not call Joe Torre?" asked Arthur Richman, a Yankees advisor who had worked with Torre on the Mets and knew him as a stand-up guy.

Steinbrenner agreed to see Torre but knew very little about him. Local newspapers knew a lot about him from his hometown connection and his failures with the Mets. When he was hired, the *New York Daily News* called him "Clueless Joe."

With or without a clue, Torre won his first pennant and World Series in 1996, missed out in 1997 and challenged Stengel and McCarthy with three straight championships in 1998, 1999 and 2000.

In 2001, the Yankees lost to the Arizona Diamondbacks when one of the game's top relievers, Mariano Rivera, couldn't hold a ninth-inning lead. The Florida Marlins beat Torre's Yankees four games to two in 2003.

Torre couldn't get the Yankees into another World Series in the next four seasons. Both sides seemed tired of each other when Torre was let go after the 2007 season. He is trying his managerial luck again with the Los Angeles Dodgers in 2008 as the kid from Brooklyn completes the rare Giants-Yankees-Dodgers cycle.

Yankee Stadium has been home to so many great players now enshrined in baseball's Hall of Fame. The managerial class from Huggins through Torre deserves equal recognition. ☐

BILLY MARTIN HAD AN OFTEN CONTENTIOUS RELATIONSHIP WITH REGGIE JACKSON.

MAURY ALLEN IS THE AUTHOR OF MORE THAN 30 BOOKS ON BASEBALL AND A LONGTIME SPORTS COLUMNIST FOR THE NEW YORK POST AND SEVERAL OTHER NEWSPAPERS. HE IS FREQUENTLY ON TELEVISION AND RADIO AS A BASEBALL COMMENTATOR AND HISTORIAN.

As owner of the New York Yankees in their first decades of glory, Jacob Ruppert was fond of saying that his ideal game was for the Yankees to score seven runs in the first inning and pull slowly ahead. Generations of Yankees fans have long applauded the sense of entitlement exuded by the wealthy Manhattan brewer and four-time United States Congressman, but it is not widely known that when Ruppert bought into the Yankees in 1915, he lamented, "We got an orphan ballclub, without a home of its own, without players of outstanding ability, without prestige."

Indeed from its inception in 1903, the team played in the shadow of John McGraw's perennially contending National League New York Giants and at times was outdrawn by the Giants' archrival Brooklyn Dodgers. The team even lacked a consistent nickname, first known as the Invaders because the franchise originated in Baltimore, and then the Highlanders because they played their games at Hilltop Park, located on one of the highest points of Manhattan. Around the time they first wore pinstripes in 1912, the Yankees became the permanent name, but a fire at Hilltop Park caused the team to move into the Polo Grounds, where they became McGraw's unwelcome tenants.

In 1915, original owners Frank Farrell, once a saloon keeper, and William S. Devery, once a police chief, had experienced enough. They sold the franchise to Ruppert and his partner, civil engineer Tillinghast L'Hommedieu Huston, for $460,000, a nice profit on their original $18,000 investment.

Success didn't come immediately for Ruppert and Huston, but after the 1919 season, prospects brightened considerably when Babe Ruth was obtained in a straight $100,000 cash deal with the Red Sox. In 1920, Ruth had a great first year in New York, hitting 54 home runs, more than any team in baseball, and for the first time in their history, the Yankees outdrew their landlords.

After the season, the Yankees made an even more important addition, signing Red Sox field manager Ed Barrow as their general manager. Though a personal friend of Boston owner Harry Frazee, Barrow saw no future in Boston, where the owner, prior to selling Ruth to the Yankees, had also shipped pitchers Dutch Leonard, Carl Mays and Ernie Shore to Gotham. Frazee later provided more great arms to New York, sending over Joe Bush, Waite Hoyt, Sam Jones and Herb Pennock as well as infielders Joe Dugan and Everett Scott.

At the age of 52, Barrow possessed experience in every aspect of the game of baseball except as a major league player. He had been a semi-pro ballplayer, concessionaire, minor league manager and president and major league manager in Detroit before becoming the Boston skipper in 1918. As Red Sox manager, he convinced Ruth that his future was best served as an everyday outfielder instead of a pitcher working only every fourth or fifth day.

Barrow knew about the importance of scouting, and he brought one of the greatest evaluators of talent, Paul Krichell, with him to New York. Specializing in college players, Krichell spotted Lou Gehrig on the Columbia College ball fields in 1923 and signed the man who became the immortal "Iron Horse." In later years, Barrow hired other able scouts like Bill Essick, Tom Greenwade and Johnny Nee. Essick recommended Joe DiMaggio and signed second baseman Joe Gordon to replace Tony Lazzeri. Greenwade signed Mickey Mantle, and Nee led the Yankees to catcher Bill Dickey.

Barrow's first three years as the man behind the pinstripes produced three straight pennant winners. After losing the first two World Series to the Giants, the Yankees turned the tables in 1923 and won the first of their 26 world championships. It was fitting that they won the crown in the year that Yankee Stadium, the world's first triple-decked stadium, opened. A monument to the grandeur

YANKEE OWNERSHIP: A HISTORY

BY: Lee Lowenfish

— YANKEE OWNERSHIP: A HISTORY —

of the Jazz Age, the 60,000-seat ballpark was completed after only 284 working days at a cost of about $2.5 million. Huston, however, was not around to celebrate the victory. The two strong personalities had never gotten along, and the previous May, Ruppert bought out his partner for more than $1.5 million. Close in age, Ruppert and Barrow became friends and worked well together. Except for negotiating top salaries like Ruth's, Ruppert let Barrow run every other aspect of the enterprise and rewarded him with a 10 percent slice of ownership.

Stability and wise choice in personnel became the hallmarks of the Ruppert-Barrow era. When manager Miller Huggins died suddenly of blood poisoning in 1929 and his first replacement, pitcher Bob Shawkey, did not work out, Barrow recommended Joe McCarthy, the former Cubs manager whose work he admired in the minor leagues. When McCarthy lost out to the Philadelphia Athletics in his rookie year of 1931, the frank and demanding Ruppert warned, "I'll stand for finishing second this year, McCarthy. But remember, I do not like to finish second." McCarthy satisfied his boss with World Series triumphs in 1932, 1936-39 and two more in 1941 and '43.

Another key component in the Yankees' success was the 1932 hiring of George Weiss as the Yankees' first farm director. Ruppert was impressed by Branch Rickey's success making the St. Louis Cardinals a dominant power through the inexpensive farm system, and he wholeheartedly endorsed Barrow's choice of Weiss, who had enjoyed outstanding success operating minor league franchises in New Haven, Conn., and Baltimore. Though Ruppert was willing to pay

for nearly finished minor league products like DiMaggio, it was the success of his farm teams in Newark, N.J., and Kansas City and his eight other affiliates that delighted the owner.

However, Ruppert wasn't around to enjoy all the success. He died in January 1939, and the bachelor owner willed the team to three nieces. When none of them wanted to assume responsibility, a bank took control of the estate, and in January 1945, a syndicate led by Larry MacPhail, Daniel Topping and Del Webb purchased the team for the remarkably low price of $2.8 million.

Topping, an Anaconda copper heir, and Webb, a California high school dropout who had made his fortune in construction and World War II government building contracts, were the money men in the group. But it was the brilliant, irascible MacPhail who became the public face of the Yankees. A pioneer in bringing night baseball to Cincinnati and Brooklyn in the 1930s, MacPhail scheduled the first night games at Yankee Stadium in 1946, spruced up the ballpark and introduced the first Stadium Club for the wealthy elite. The Yankees became the first team in baseball history to draw more than 2 million fans.

The holdovers from the Ruppert era, McCarthy, Barrow and Weiss were aghast at MacPhail's flamboyant style. McCarthy resigned as manager early in the 1946 season. Barrow was only a ceremonial chairman of the board, and he was eased into retirement before dying in 1953. At a party after the Yankees' 1947 World Series triumph over the Dodgers, MacPhail fired Weiss in a hot-tempered, rage.

Soon after, though, MacPhail suddenly announced his own retirement from baseball. Topping and Webb quickly

BABE RUTH, ED BARROW AND JACOB RUPPERT BROUGHT SUCCESS TO THE YANKEES.

— YANKEE OWNERSHIP: A HISTORY —

reinstated Weiss, and starting in 1949, a remarkable new Yankees dynasty commenced. For the next 16 years, the team won 14 pennants and nine World Series.

Meanwhile, in 1953, Topping and Webb sold their interest in Yankee Stadium to Arnold Johnson, a Chicago real estate mogul who bought the Philadelphia Athletics and moved them to Kansas City the following year. To avoid a palpable conflict of interest, baseball commissioner Ford Frick ordered Johnson to sell his interest in the ballpark. But in the next few years, Johnson's activities were reminiscent of Frazee's Red Sox fire sales. The Kansas City owner supplied the Yankees with star performers like third baseman Clete Boyer, relief ace Ryne Duren and future home run king Roger Maris. After the Yankees lost a hard-fought World Series to the Pirates in 1960, Topping and Webb fired Stengel and Weiss, ostensibly because of their advanced ages.

Though the Yankees won the next four American League pennants, it was a last gasp for that dynasty. From 1965 to 1975, the Yankees came full circle, back to the days when they were the second-class citizen in town. After the new Shea Stadium opened in Queens in 1964, the Mets became the darlings of New York fans, especially after they shocked the world by winning the 1969 World Series. Yankees attendance fell under a million for the first time since World War II.

Meanwhile, Topping and Webb had sold the team in the summer of 1964 to the Columbia Broadcasting System for the record amount of $11.2 million. CBS installed Michael Burke, a former Ivy League college football star, as team president. However, Burke inherited an aging team and a farm system that was drying up, especially as new rules initiated an amateur free agent draft that prevented the stockpiling of prospects by any one team.

CBS grew increasingly dissatisfied with its investment, and in January 1973, it cut its losses by selling the team for approximately $10 million to a syndicate headed by Cleveland shipbuilder George M. Steinbrenner III.

"We plan absentee ownership," Steinbrenner said upon buying the team. "I'll stick to running ships." Of course, just as Barrow wasn't given any role with the MacPhail Yankees, Steinbrenner soon dismissed Burke as the president and took on that mantle himself with the assistance of veteran baseball man Gabe Paul.

Steinbrenner was quickly dubbed "George III" by the avid New York media for his imperious style and passionate commitment to winning. In 1976, the Yankees returned to a renovated Yankee Stadium, and history repeated itself. The team won the pennant in their spruced-up ballpark, a product of more than $100 million in city government expenditures.

Though they were swept by the Reds in the World Series, the Yankees returned to win back-to-back titles over the Dodgers in 1977 and '78. Fans flocked to see a team that was dubbed "the Bronx Zoo" for the constant controversy fueled by owner Steinbrenner, his volatile free agent acquisition Reggie Jackson and combative manager Billy Martin. Sportswriter Ed Linn described their relationship as "like three scorpions in a bottle in a ritual dance of sting and embrace."

Still, despite a World Series appearance in 1981, the Yankees were barren of a world title from 1979 to 1995, the longest stretch without a championship since moving to Yankee Stadium. In 1995, the Yankees returned to postseason play and have remained there, a constant contender despite not having won a World Series since 2000.

By 2007, Steinbrenner had become more of an emeritus owner as his two sons, Hank and Hal, assumed more active roles in ownership. Farm system development has taken priority again as Hal Steinbrenner has sided with general manager Brian Cashman on the need to avoid expensive free agent contracts. Still, the insistence on winning championships remains the top priority.

Somewhere in the great beyond, Ruppert is nodding his enthusiastic approval. ☐

"WE PLAN ABSENTEE OWNERSHIP. I'LL STICK TO RUNNING SHIPS."

— GEORGE STEINBRENNER —

LEE LOWENFISH'S LATEST BOOK IS "BRANCH RICKEY: BASEBALL'S FEROCIOUS GENTLEMAN" PUBLISHED BY THE UNIVERSITY OF NEBRASKA PRESS. HE HAS ALSO WRITTEN ABOUT BROOKS ROBINSON AND TOM SEAVER FOR RECENT PRESSBOX LEGENDS PUBLICATIONS.

TRADITION BY POSITION

BY: Maury Allen

With a streak of 56 consecutive games with a hit in 1941, Joe DiMaggio was dubbed baseball's greatest living player. Although not everyone agreed, it was all about tradition by position.

The Yankees dominated baseball with 39 pennants and 26 World Series titles from 1921 through 2003, seemingly always anchored by superior center fielders. The vast space in Yankee Stadium, as much as 490 feet in center field from 1923 through 1936 and then shortened to 461 feet, was a test for any of the outer gardeners.

If distance wasn't enough for the Yankees' center fielders, the challenge of monuments placed on the field in the deepest recesses added to the test.

Detroit slugger Hank Greenberg, challenging Babe Ruth's single-season home run record with 58 in 1938, once blasted a ball that DiMaggio caught behind the monuments, 450 feet from home plate. He wasn't the only DiMaggio to catch one behind the monuments for manager Miller Huggins and owner Jacob Ruppert. Kid brother Dom DiMaggio of the Boston Red Sox collared one of his older brother's shots in the same area.

No fewer than three center fielders, Joe DiMaggio, Mickey Mantle and Earle Combs, earned Hall of Fame credentials with their incredible play on that lush green grass and blasts at the plate.

It is DiMaggio, of course, who remains the standard of center field excellence.

"In all the years I had him out there, he never made a mistake," manager Joe McCarthy said. "He didn't have to catch baseballs in a spectacular way. He always knew where the ball was and glided over to it."

"He was the best the game ever had," manager Casey Stengel said after DiMaggio retired in 1951. "You could go to the moon, and you won't find a better center fielder."

DiMaggio didn't feel quite as warm toward Stengel, his last manager in his final seasons. DiMaggio had slowed down a great deal in his final season, and his arm was a liability. Stengel tried to duck the issue by moving DiMaggio to first base for one game.

"I didn't like that," DiMaggio said coldly. He was soon back in center field, but a leaked report by Brooklyn scout Andy High was published just before the 1951 World Series. It included the phrase, "Run on him as much as possible."

While Ruth and Lou Gehrig were getting most of the offensive attention for the Yankees in the 1920s and into the early '30s, it was Combs who protected the center field acres.

Combs, a smooth, graceful outfielder with a strong arm, hit .325 from 1924 to 1935 with no less than nine years of hitting over .300 in his 12 seasons. He could run well and was often the table-setter for the thundering Yankees teams, especially the 1927 juggernaut, for which he collected a league-

> ## "IN ALL THE YEARS I HAD [JOE DIMAGGIO] OUT THERE, HE NEVER MADE A MISTAKE."
>
> — JOE MCCARTHY —

— TRADITION BY POSITION —

leading 231 hits with a .356 average. Detroit's Harry Heilmann won the batting title that year with a .398 mark.

Ruth hit his 60 homers that year, and Gehrig added 47, the standard for a home run tandem until Roger Maris and Mantle raised the bar in 1961. Combs didn't get much attention on a team many experts consider the best in the history of the game.

———————————— ★ ————————————

Ben Chapman and Jake Powell filled the gap between Combs and DiMaggio.

DiMaggio arrived on the scene in 1936 from San Francisco with his 61-game consecutive hitting streak and a bad knee. McCarthy started him slowly in left field but soon moved him into the spacious center field position. Center field remained DiMaggio's home through 1951, except for the war years of 1943-1945.

A kid named Mantle, all of 19 years old, played right field in the 1951 World Series against the New York Giants. In the second game, another rookie named Willie Mays hit a fly ball to right-center. Mantle drifted to his right for the catch, but DiMaggio was moving over to his left.

"Joe had told me before the game that I was to take everything between us," Mantle once said. "His legs were bad and he was slowing down. I went for the ball and suddenly heard Joe call out, 'I got it.' I just stopped."

The sudden stop cost Mantle his famous speed. His right leg got caught in a drainage ditch, and he had to undergo surgery at New York's Lenox Hill Hospital.

He never again had an explosive charge out of the box.

Mantle came back strong in 1952, took over DiMaggio's center field spot, went on to a rare Triple Crown season in 1956 and became the game's greatest switch hitter over 18 seasons.

After the 1968 season, Mantle retired with a .298 lifetime average and 536 homers. He was also one of the game's premier bunters, especially from the left side.

MICKEY MANTLE CONTINUED THE STRONG LEGACY OF YANKEES CENTER FIELDERS AFTER JOE DIMAGGIO'S RETIREMENT.

"Whenever I was in a slump, I would just lay one down," he once said. "I usually could beat them out. That would get me off the 'oh-fer,' and I would relax and start hitting again."

Mostly he hit huge drives, like the mythical 565-foot homer off Washington's Chuck Stobbs and the blast against the right field facade off Kansas City's Bill Fischer.

"That was my hardest shot, but my favorite home run was the one I hit in the 1964 [World] Series off the reliever Barney Schultz on his first pitch," Mantle said of the shot that won Game 3.

In 1965, Mantle began showing signs of slowing down. His wear and tear over the years, his vigorous lifestyle and his weak legs caught up with him. He hit only 82 homers in his final four seasons and fell to a career-low .237 average in his last year. He also couldn't cover center quickly enough, and manager Ralph Houk moved him to first base.

———————————— ★ ————————————

Mantle struggled with the bat and the first baseman's glove over those last two seasons. He was soon helping another kid from Oklahoma, Bobby Murcer, take over the position he had protected for 16 glorious summers.

Murcer, like Mantle, came to the Yankees as a shortstop. His baby face and 5-foot-10, 160-pound frame could not compare with Mantle's 5-foot-11, 195-pound muscular frame. Murcer had the burden of succeeding Mantle as Mantle did in succeeding DiMaggio.

"I think the difference was Mickey took me under his wing and tried to help me as much as he could," Murcer said. "I don't think Joe ever did that with Mickey."

Despite his relatively small frame, Murcer had a smooth swing and a perfect left-handed stroke. He hit 25 home runs in 1971, 33 the following season and 22 in 1973.

In 1974, the Yankees moved to Shea Stadium, home of the crosstown New York Mets, as Yankee Stadium underwent a complete remodeling. In the larger confines of Shea with its higher wall and nasty winds, Murcer dropped to only 10 homers. He was dispatched to San Francisco, where he hit 11 home runs in 1975 and 23 in '76.

Murcer returned to the Yankees as a center fielder and then as a designated hitter and pinch hitter in 1979. He made a World Series appearance in 1981, lasted into the 1983 season and ended his career with a .277 mark and 252 home runs.

One of the most popular players of his time, Murcer protected center field with honor over 12 seasons before he became a broadcaster with the team. He made a courageous comeback on the air during the 2007 season despite a serious bout with brain cancer.

★

BERNIE WILLIAMS COVERED CENTER FIELD FOR THE YANKEES FROM 1991 TO 2006.

———— ★ ————

The Yankees searched for a center fielder for the next decade after Murcer gave up the position. Few could handle the vast territory.

The Yankees didn't win anything after 1981 until 1996. A lot of the responsibility for the lost years fell on the shoulders of the also-rans who chased after lost baseballs in the area made famous by Combs, DiMaggio, Mantle and Murcer.

In 1985, the Yankees signed a soft-spoken 17-year-old from Puerto Rico who loved baseball and his guitar with equal intensity.

Bernie Williams had a slow, difficult climb to Yankees stardom. His self-effacing personality seemed to keep him hidden in the Yankees chain.

Williams made it to the parent club in 1991 as a graceful switch hitter without the power of Mantle or the confidence of DiMaggio. He was in and out of the lineup for two years due to inconsistency, his inability to use his running speed to his advantage and his weak throwing arm.

Manager Buck Showalter won a battle with George Steinbrenner when ownership wanted to move Williams out of Yankee Stadium for a harder hitting outfielder. They could find none.

The Yankees won their first pennant in 15 years in 1996, and Williams hit a home run against the Atlanta Braves in the third game of the World Series

— TRADITION BY POSITION —

to set the Yankees up for four straight wins and their first title since 1978. After that, he was on his way to stardom.

In 1998, Williams won a batting title with a .339 mark, protected the green grass with his Gold Glove and earned his second World Series ring. The Yankees went 114-48 that season, and much of the credit went to Williams, who had quietly developed into a team leader without the flair of shortstop and captain Derek Jeter.

Despite his evasive personality and his constant locker room performances on his guitar, many with the accompaniment of teammate Paul O'Neill on drums, Williams was gaining attention as the equal successor to the previous legendary center fielders of the Yankees.

He accumulated 2,336 hits as a lifetime Yankee, smashed 286 homers, had a career average of .297 and an enviable postseason mark of appearing in a record 121 games.

★

"MICKEY [MANTLE] TOOK ME UNDER HIS WING AND TRIED TO HELP ME AS MUCH AS HE COULD."

— BOBBY MURCER —

★

In the spring of 2007, after his contract expired, the Yankees asked Williams to come to Tampa and win a job with the club. Instead, he held out for a guaranteed contract, something the Yankees refused to offer the 38-year-old outfielder.

Williams stayed in shape but never received a call to join any other team as a contract player. Instead, he performed publicly on the guitar, followed the Yankees on television and enjoyed life at home with his wife and three children.

"I don't know what the future holds," he said. "I am enjoying being away from the game, just doing what I'm doing now."

Williams fits snugly into the pantheon of Yankee center fielders, along with Combs, DiMaggio, Mantle and Murcer.

Tradition by position. They all filled it nobly. □

MAURY ALLEN IS THE AUTHOR OF MORE THAN 30 BOOKS ON BASEBALL AND A LONGTIME SPORTS COLUMNIST FOR THE NEW YORK POST AND SEVERAL OTHER NEWSPAPERS. HE IS FREQUENTLY ON TELEVISION AND RADIO AS A BASEBALL COMMENTATOR AND HISTORIAN.

★ |  YANKEES
BATTING CHAMPIONS

A YANKEE HAS LED THE AMERICAN LEAGUE IN BATTING NINE TIMES.

YEAR	PLAYER	AVG.	YEAR	PLAYER	AVG.
1998	BERNIE WILLIAMS	.339	1940	JOE DIMAGGIO	.352
1994	PAUL O'NEILL	.359	1939	JOE DIMAGGIO	.381
1984	DON MATTINGLY	.343	1934	LOU GEHRIG	.363
1956	MICKEY MANTLE	.353	1924	BABE RUTH	.378
1945	SNUFFY STIRNWEISS	.309		*Through 2007 season*	

ankee Stadium was an equal opportunity field of dreams. Let's imagine she could talk. Listen in:

"Here are some of the men who played here: Jim Brown, Johnny Unitas, the New York Giants and the Green Bay Packers, Doc Blanchard and Glenn Davis, Johnny Lujack and the Seven Blocks of Granite.

"And the men who coached here – for starters, how about Knute Rockne, Eddie Robinson and Vince Lombardi? Not bad for a baseball park, right?"

Lombardi, for whom the Super Bowl trophy is named, also played at Yankee Stadium. Along with Leo Paquin, Johnny Druze, Alex Wojciechowicz, Ed Franco, Al Babartsky and Natty Pierce, he was part of the Fordham University offensive

molded with the Giants by Landry. "They actually competed against each other. [The defensive players] had our own dressing room – and the offense was not allowed in the area. We just about hated the offense."

Those Giants were the first to receive the fame defensive units throughout the NFL had long deserved. Huff made the cover of *Time* magazine in 1959 and was the subject of one of the initial television programs about NFL players, called "The Violent World of Sam Huff." All that began when the Giants moved from the Polo Grounds before the '56 season.

"When we switched to Yankee Stadium, it was like going from the outhouse to the penthouse," said Giants Hall of Fame runner/receiver Frank Gifford. "First thing I did was look around at all those [baseball] monuments. I couldn't believe we were there. … Nobody seemed to care about us at

LEGACY ON THE GRIDIRON

BY: Ken Denlinger

line known in the mid-1930s as the Seven Blocks of Granite. Fordham was a national power at that time, and its games with then-mighty New York University routinely drew upward of 75,000 to Yankee Stadium.

Lombardi coached in Yankee Stadium before building the Packers into an NFL dynasty in the 1960s. He was an assistant on some of Red Blaik's best Army teams that frequently played at Yankee Stadium, although not the ones that featured Blanchard and Davis, each of whom won the Heisman Trophy.

With the New York Giants teams that started using Yankee Stadium in 1956, Lombardi was half of the most illustrious pair of assistants in NFL history. Few remember the Giants' head coach during the mid- and late 1950s, Jim Lee Howell. However, even casual NFL historians know that Lombardi ran the offense and that the defense was prepped by Tom Landry, whose later work as coach of the Dallas Cowboys puts him among contenders to join Lombardi if the NFL ever creates its coaching version of Mount Rushmore.

"We knew how great those two were," said Sam Huff, whose career as a Hall of Fame middle linebacker was

the Polo Grounds. All of a sudden, we were heroes."

That's because all of a sudden, the '56 Giants became NFL champions, beating the Chicago Bears, 47-7, in Yankee Stadium. The last time the Giants had won the world title was in 1938.

———————— ————————

Lombardi's Packers also won the 1962 NFL title in Yankee Stadium, beating the Giants, 16-7, in one of the coldest football games ever. Huff's helmet from that game made it to the Pro Football Hall of Fame before he did. It's there because of a dent caused by Huff and Packers fullback Jim Taylor colliding in the manner of rams rutting.

"I knocked him out at about the 20-yard line," Huff said. "I was dazed. Someone said Taylor swallowed his tongue."

In truth, Taylor bit his tongue and was spitting blood when he came to the Packers' sideline, where Dave Anderson, who later won the Pulitzer Prize for his work as a sports columnist for the *New York Times*, happened to be standing.

"Blood was coming out of his mouth," Anderson said. "I was standing next to him. For maybe 30 seconds, he was spitting blood. The Packers defense held, and the Giants

— LEGACY ON THE GRIDIRON —

were about to punt, and we suddenly heard this loud voice, Lombardi's. 'TAYLOR, TAYLOR, TAYLOR.' Taylor spat blood another time, grabbed his helmet and went back on the field."

The Huff-Taylor collision, though nearly unique in its ferocity, was outdone in lore by at least two others in Yankee Stadium. The first, oddly enough, was initiated by a quarterback, Notre Dame's Lujack, a two-time All-American and Heisman Trophy winner in 1947. Lujack later became prominent in the NFL as a defensive back with the Bears, and his prowess as a tackler was established during No. 2 Notre Dame's 0-0 tie with No. 1 Army in 1946.

Army was a heavy favorite that day, and Blanchard seemed to be headed for the winning touchdown until Lujack nailed him with an open-field tackle.

That game drew 74,000 fans to Yankee Stadium and had countless other fans throughout the country rooting intently while listening to the radio. Some high school football players in upstate New York took a portable radio and planted it on the bench before their game with an overmatched opponent.

"We cared more about that game," said one of the players, Ned Taylor, "than we did about the one we were playing."

The other momentous tackle, which topped even Huff's on Taylor and is widely regarded as the most famous in the NFL, came Nov. 20, 1960, near what was the pitcher's mound in Yankee Stadium. The Giants' Gifford went over the middle and, immediately after he made a spectacular catch, Philadelphia Eagles linebacker

Chuck Bednarik leveled him with a vicious, though perfectly legal, tackle. The Eagles were assured victory after they recovered the fumble Bednarik's hit caused.

"That was the best hit or the worst hit, depending on how you want to say it, that I've ever seen in sports," Huff said. "I thought he'd killed him."

Gifford left the field on a stretcher shortly before the game ended. By unfortunate coincidence, according to Huff, a security guard at Yankee Stadium had suffered a heart attack and died around the time Bednarik popped Gifford. And when his body, completely covered with a sheet, was carried past several Giants players near the locker room at game's end, Huff thought, "There goes Frank. He's dead."

Gifford was alive, of course, but did not play the entire 1961 season. Most fans assumed it was because of Bednarik's hit, which caused a spinal concussion.

GIANTS KYLE ROTE (SECOND FROM LEFT), NO. 16 FRANK GIFFORD AND NO. 42 CHARLIE CONERLY CALLED YANKEE STADIUM HOME.

Gifford said he had simply retired after the '60 season, figuring it was time to devote his energy to the broadcast work he had done while playing with the Giants.

"I could have played in '61," he said.

While working in radio and television during the '61 season, Gifford often joined his former teammates at practice and discovered, "I could still beat them in pass patterns." Gifford returned to action in 1962 and made the Pro Bowl in 1963 at a third position, wide receiver.

Levity on the playing field is not usually associated with the NFL, but the Baltimore Colts provided some during an exhibition with the Giants in Yankee Stadium. The versatile

— LEGACY ON THE GRIDIRON —

Tom Matte recalled that free-spirited linebacker Don Shinnick, near the end of a Baltimore blowout, bought a hot dog from a vendor operating near the Colts' bench.

Before Shinnick could take a bite, however, the Colts' defense had to hustle back on the field, so he handed the hot dog to teammate Roy Hilton. When Shinnick retuned to the bench, Hilton had eaten the hot dog.

★

Of the nearly 200 college and other amateur football games played in Yankee Stadium, beginning with Syracuse edging Pittsburgh, 3-0, in 1923 and ending with Central State of Ohio beating Eddie Robinson's Grambling team, 37-21, in 1987, none has lingered more in the minds of Americans than Notre Dame vs. Army in 1928. The game was as fierce as anyone had seen at the time, but it became a significant part of American culture because of some three dozen words Rockne told his Notre Dame team.

It's the most famous locker room speech in history, delivered in cramped, cold dressing quarters to players badly in need of high-octane inspiration, and the phrase that still lingers is, "Win one for the Gipper." Although the audience numbered no more than several dozen, what was said ranks up there in Yankee Stadium vocal memories with Lou Gehrig's "I consider myself the luckiest man on the face of this earth."

Under Rockne, Notre Dame had ascended from an obscure Indiana Catholic university to the most famous football factory in the country – and, starting at the Polo Grounds, New York played an important part in that rise. It was the Broadway of college football, which, at the time, was far more popular than the pro game.

And after it was built in 1923, Yankee Stadium started replacing the Polo Grounds as the place to play in New York. NYU and Fordham drew crowds of 78,000 for their games in 1930 and '31; the Notre Dame-Army games frequently lured more than 80,000. Two Army-Navy games, 1930 and '31, were held there.

The Gipper, of course, was George Gipp, an all-around whiz from Michigan's upper peninsula who amassed more than 4,100 yards rushing and passing and 150 points on touchdowns, extra points and field goals.

According to Murray Sperber's "Shake Down the Thunder: The Creation of Notre Dame Football," the authenticity of Gipp's last words is difficult to pin down. For instance, no one called him Gipper, nor did he ever refer to himself that way. Moreover, Rockne was not at Gipp's deathbed; he did visit Gipp during his final weeks in 1920, but they were rarely alone.

But motivation was clearly needed for the Army game in '28. Notre Dame came in with a 4-3 record. According to Rockne's version, which didn't appear until two years later in *Collier's* magazine, Gipp said, "I've got to go, Rock. It's all right. I'm not afraid. Some time, when the team's up against it; when things are wrong and the breaks are beating the boys – tell them to go in there with all they've got and win just one for the Gipper. I don't know where I'll be then, Rock. But I'll know about it, and I'll be happy."

Army broke the 0-0 halftime score with a touchdown. But Notre Dame won, 12-6, inspired by Rockne's speech.

The Gipper speech was a highlight of the 1940 biopic "Knute Rockne: All-American," over which Rockne's wife Bonnie had complete editorial control, and Sperber speculates about what it meant to the man who played Gipp, Ronald Reagan: "Would [he] have been as successful [in becoming the president of the United States], particularly in appealing to the crucial vote of 'Reagan Democrats' – many of them Catholic – without his appealing campaign slogan, 'Win one for the Gipper?'"

★

Yankee Stadium, Dec. 28, 1958. Before the Baltimore Colts kicked off to the New York Giants, nobody anticipated anything close to what would happen when the weeks after the game melted into years and the years

"WHEN WE SWITCHED TO YANKEE STADIUM, IT WAS LIKE GOING FROM THE OUTHOUSE TO THE PENTHOUSE."

— FRANK GIFFORD —

— LEGACY ON THE GRIDIRON —

became close to a half-century, that this match for the NFL championship would turn pro football toward becoming America's sporting passion.

It's true that about 45 million people watched on television, the largest such audience for an NFL game up to that time. It's also true that the game was far less than a sellout, causing it to be blacked out in New York City. Still, many experienced a unique thrill.

"When [the teams] got introduced and my name came up, I said, 'Jesus, I never thought I'd be in this situation,'" said former Colts defensive tackle Art Donovan, who grew up in the Bronx. "Because as a kid, in none of my wildest dreams would I think I'd be introduced at Yankee Stadium."

Pro football had been a small part of Yankee Stadium prior to the Giants' move there before the '56 season, and Donovan had been involved. Teams calling themselves the New York Yankees were in the NFL in 1926 and '27 and in rival leagues during the 1930s and '40s. The Yanks returned to the NFL in 1950 and '51, and Donovan was one of the defensive linemen.

The team folded in 1951, and Donovan went along when they became the Dallas Texans. And when the Texans folded in '52, Donovan also went along when they became the Baltimore Colts the next year.

In all, 16 men involved in that '58 title game would be enshrined in the Pro Football Hall of Fame – 12 players, including Donovan, plus Lombardi, Landry and Colts head coach Weeb Eubank. The 16th was Giants owner Wellington Mara, and one of his assignments during the '50s seems ludicrous to modern fans.

Mara, according to Huff, would take Polaroid pictures of the opponents' defense from the roof of Yankee Stadium, fold them into a tube and then shoot that tube down a wire to the bench.

Huff was the featured player on those Giants defenses, Landry devising a scheme that sort of funneled ball carriers toward him. And Huff relished it.

"I probably had more knockouts than the heavyweight champion of the world," he said.

Also vivid to Huff is a collision between Cleveland's Brown and Huff's smallish Giants teammate, defensive back Dick Nolan.

COACH TOM LANDRY DIAGRAMS A PLAY IN THE STADIUM LOCKER ROOM, WHERE YANKEES PHOTOS DECORATE THE WALLS.

"I thought Jim Brown had killed him," Huff said. "But Nolan made the tackle. I go over and pick Nolan up. His eyes are back in his head. I say, 'That was a great tackle! You got him all by yourself!' He looked at me and said, 'Great tackle. Hell, Sam, I couldn't get out of his way.'"

Unfortunately for Huff and the Giants, the nonpareil Unitas got out of their way at all the crucial times that seminal Sunday and, in overtime, the Colts edged the Giants, 23-17.

"John would whistle it right by your ear," Huff said about the quarterback. "He looked like he was throwing it right at you, but he'd put it where you couldn't put your arm up to block it. ... I thought he could read my mind, so I would always call two different defenses in the huddle, thinking I could throw him off."

The Giants left Yankee Stadium for the Meadowlands in New Jersey more than three decades before Yankee Stadium left us. And near the end, Huff made a stay-of-execution plea that went unheeded.

"To me, Yankee Stadium is a monument of the people, by the people, for the people, so to speak," he said. "I don't think this country tears down monuments." □

KEN DENLINGER COVERED A VARIETY OF SPORTS FOR THE WASHINGTON POST FOR 38 YEARS.

ost people's grasp of history is such that they think Joan of Arc was Noah's wife. It's even worse when it comes to the history of sports. For instance, very few sports fans know that Yankee Stadium has had almost as many great moments in boxing as it has had in baseball.

Go back, if you will, to three months after Yankee Stadium opened in April 1923 to July 23, when the great lightweight title bout between Benny Leonard and Lew Tendler drew a record 70,000 fans.

Over the next half-century, Yankee Stadium played host to more than 40 unforgettable fights, including Joe Louis-Billy Conn, Tony Zale-Rocky Graziano, Joey Maxim-Sugar Ray Robinson, Carmen Basilio-Robinson, Sandy Saddler-Willie

who would not only blow away the rest of the heavyweights but revitalize the sport.

Louis was accorded a special place in boxing as a superhero by his enthusiastic fans, who viewed him as invincible, and by the press, who believed he was the most dependable story in sports. But after 27 straight wins, 23 of those by knockout, the man called the "Brown Bomber" was matched with former heavyweight champion Schmeling, brought out of retirement to serve as yet another sacrificial lamb.

No one gave the former titleholder much of a chance, the bettors included, who made Schmeling a 10-to-1 underdog. But he was an underdog with a plan. He had been an onlooker at the earlier Louis-Paulino Uzcudun fight and afterward flashed a Mona Lisa-like smile and muttered something that sounded like "I zee some things."

A BACKDROP TO BOXING

★ BY: Bert Randolph Sugar

Pep, Ingemar Johansson-Floyd Patterson, Rocky Marciano-Archie Moore, Muhammad Ali-Ken Norton.

But the greatest fight ever held at Yankee Stadium and one of the greatest sports events in history occurred on the night of June 22, 1938, when Louis sought to avenge his lone defeat two years earlier at the hands of Max Schmeling. The fight was not just a fight, it was a harbinger of the war to come pitting Schmeling, the symbol of Aryan supremacy, against Louis, democracy's and America's flag bearer.

That night, more than 70,000 screaming fans watched Louis destroy the myth of Aryan might. Babe Ruth's 60th home run, Roger Maris' 61st, Don Larsen's perfect game pale in comparison, both in excitement and historic meaning. Here is the story of Yankee Stadium's most memorable event:

Ring archeologists can date the end of the golden age of boxing back to the retirements of Jack Dempsey and Gene Tunney. Behind them came a group of nondescript, almost comical, heavyweight champions, including the likes of Primo Carnera, Max Baer and Jack Sharkey. But even as boxing was on the cusp of being called off on account of lack of interest, along came a whirlwind out of the Midwest named Joe Louis,

What Schmeling had seen was that after Louis had thrown a left jab, he had dropped his left hand, leaving himself wide open for an overhand right. And on the night of the fight, Schmeling, determined to take the advantage of the chink he had seen in Louis' armament, came out with his chin tucked deep into his left shoulder, his right eye exposed to Louis' left in order to deliver his own right hand.

In the second round, when Louis initiated his first left, Schmeling came across with a smashing right to the chin, dazing Louis. That would be the first of 54 times Schmeling would cross his right over Louis's lazy left, finally knocking out the myth in the 12th round.

For most fighters, a knockout loss such as that suffered by Louis would have been devastating, their confidence destroyed. But not in the case of Louis, who came back within two months to knock out another ex-champion, Sharkey. Then, almost one year to the day after his destruction at the fists of Schmeling, Louis won the heavyweight championship of the world by knocking out Jimmy Braddock.

Part of the ritual of becoming the heavyweight champion is promising to be a fighting champion. Louis had promised it,

— A BACKDROP TO BOXING —

and he meant it. Two months after dethroning Braddock, he was back in the ring fighting Tommy Farr. After decisioning Farr, he went on to knock out Natie Mann and Harry Thomas. After each victory, Louis acted like a man possessed, telling everyone within earshot, "Bring on Max Schmeling. Bring him on…" On June 22, 1938, two years and three days after his loss to Schmeling, he got his wish.

The bout was viewed by most Americans as a contest between two ideologies, Louis wearing the colors of all Americans against the representative of the National Socialist, or Nazi, Party. Even President Franklin Roosevelt got into the act, inviting Louis to the White House, where he gripped his biceps and said, "Joe, we're depending on those muscles for America."

The scene outside Yankee Stadium the night of the fight was a veritable mob scene, one reminiscent of the worst excesses of the French Revolution. Some 70,000 fans had to pass through picket lines set up outside the stadium by the Anti-Nazi League, most carrying posters reading "Oust Hitler's Agents and Spies" or "Down with Hitler." Inside, Louis warmed up in his dressing room for 30 minutes instead of his normal 10.

Almost before the reverberating echoes of ring announcer Harry Balough's pre-fight oratory had died down, Louis emerged from his corner to meet Schmeling more than halfway across the ring and within five seconds had landed a spearing left, the first of what mathematicians counted as 50 blows. Schmeling got in his first lick, an arching right to the jaw. This time, instead of reeling under its impact, Louis merely sneered and stepped in with his own right to the jaw, propelling Schmeling back into the ropes, his body half-turned. Louis leaped in and landed a thudding right to Schmeling's unprotected rib cage, causing the challenger to let out an audible shriek that sounded like a wounded animal caught in a trap.

Then came a bewildering succession of powerful rights and lefts to Schmeling's head as the German began to crumble, his face twisted in a grotesque mask. Suddenly Louis sent in a vicious right and Schmeling toppled.

Somewhere between the first knockdown and the third knockdown, the radio broadcast of the fight back to Germany was mysteriously interrupted, courtesy of the propaganda officer assigned to the broadcast by Herr Doktor Goebbels. No one in Germany was to know the outcome, at least officially, until the papers black-bordered it the following morning.

The millions of listeners surrounding their radios in America heard it loud and clear, the gravelly voice of ringside announcer Clem McCarthy shouting, "A right and left to the head … A left to the jaw … A right to the head … And referee Donovan is watching carefully … Louis measures him … Right to the body, a left hook to the jaw … And Schmeling is down … The count is five … five … six … seven … eight … Men are in the ring … The fight is over on a technical knockout … Max Schmeling is beaten in one round."

Louis had avenged his loss to Schmeling with a 124-second annihilation that would set back the cause of the so-called "master race" and bring joy to millions of Americans in the most historic fight in boxing annals. It was one of the greatest events ever at Yankee Stadium. ☐

★

JOE LOUIS KNOCKS DOWN MAX SCHMELING AT
YANKEE STADIUM ON JUNE 22, 1938.

A LEGENDARY BOXING WRITER AND MEMBER OF THE BOXING HALL OF FAME, BERT RANDOLPH SUGAR HAS EDITED THE RING, BOXING ILLUSTRATED AND FIGHT GAME MAGAZINES AND WRITTEN OVER 80 BOOKS, INCLUDING "THE 100 GREATEST BOXERS OF ALL TIME."

When Pope Paul VI visited New York in 1965, it marked the first time a reigning pontiff spent time on American soil.

As the *New York Times* noted Sept. 11, 1965, "More important, it will be the first time in history a pope has addressed a gathering of political leaders representing the political, ideological and spiritual families of mankind."

For such auspicious purposes, Yankee Stadium offered the perfect venue to reach the largest audience. The stadium was designed to accommodate a crowd of 70,000 for special events. With chairs on the infield and other modifications, capacity expanded well beyond that.

Indeed, on the evening of Oct. 4 of that year, Pope Paul

5 p.m. stood clad in warm coats, huddled together," the *Times* reported. "Many had forgotten to wear gloves and blew on their hands or clasped hot containers of coffee in both hands."

Specifically, the Pope stood 171 feet from home plate as he spoke before the thousands gathered at the stadium. A collection of gold and white chrysanthemums and greens surrounded a 6-foot high stage that held the pulpit.

Pope Paul VI arrived at Yankee Stadium in an open convertible. The car was driven through the gate of the left field bullpen, where only a few days before, on Sept. 26, American League "Fireman of the Year" Eddie Fisher emerged to pitch the final two innings of the Yankees' home finale, earning the save in a 5-3 win for the Chicago White Sox.

From there, Paul VI offered the mass in Latin. However,

THE PAPAL VISITS

BY: Mike Lurie

addressed 90,000 worshippers at Yankee Stadium, urging them "to love and serve a peace based on 'moral and religious principles,'" according to the *Times*.

His celebration of mass at Yankee Stadium is one of three such historic visits that Yankee Stadium has hosted. Pope John Paul II celebrated mass at the stadium in 1979 and Pope Benedict VI stood before worshippers April 20, 2008.

Whereas a Yankees game at the time would have the traditional surroundings of T-shirt and pennant vendors, the entrepreneurs around the Grand Concourse hawked different wares: statues of the Infant of Prague, rosaries and buttons with the Pope's likeness.

Remember, too, that Yankee Stadium had no shortage of advertising in place for Yankees games. Those ads were obscured "by hundreds of yards of billowing blue cloth," the *Times* noted.

Where banners reading "Tigers" or "Athletics" normally flew from the upper deck circumference, flags of assorted United Nations countries flapped in the wind.

"In the outfield, in front of the bleachers, a picket fence was used to rope off an area for students, who as early as

as the crowd gathered under the Yankee Stadium lights, it read responses and sang in English.

For a brief time, the Pope did speak in English. He said to the crowd, "Brothers and sons of New York, brothers and sons of the United Nations and of all America, all of you who have assembled here from every part of the world, we greet you and we bless you."

There was no shortage of religious leaders on site who were non-Catholics, including Norman Vincent Peale (president of the Protestant Council of New York), Simon Greenberg (vice chancellor of the Jewish Theological Seminary) and Archbishop Iakovos (primate of the Greek Orthodox Church).

The 1965 visit to the stadium was part of a New York trip during which the Pope's stated purpose was to speak before the U.N. General Assembly and plead for world peace. According to the *Times*, that mission was accomplished at the United Nations as "Pope Paul's visit and address on behalf of world peace brought a unanimity of warm response virtually unknown here."

The Pope also visited St. Patrick's Cathedral that day. And,

— THE PAPAL VISITS —

through a thorny and complex set of loopholes surrounding protocol over the fact that Vatican City is not a member of the United Nations, the Pope managed to encounter President Lyndon Johnson that evening while avoiding certain bureaucratic rituals often required during visits between heads of state.

Joseph Zwilling, director of the office of communications at the Archdiocese of New York, said that Yankee Stadium will always hold a distinct place in the history of papal visits to the United States.

"There has been no place in our country that has hosted more than one mass with our Holy Father, except for Yankee Stadium," Zwilling said. "It's especially fitting that the third visit was to come in this last season for the stadium. I think it's a tremendous blessing for the Archdiocese of New York that we have a place like Yankee Stadium available to use for these kinds of events."

To add more color to his appreciation, Zwilling recalled the late Yankees announcer Mel Allen, the radio voice most identified with the franchise's lore.

"Mel Allen once called St. Patrick's Cathedral the Yankee Stadium of churches," Zwilling said. "There is a long and rich history between the Archdiocese and the Yankees."

Allen himself was Jewish. But he was a close personal friend of Cardinal Spellman, the Archbishop of New York. At the end of each baseball season, Allen made sure the Yankees' season highlight film was delivered to the Pontifical North American College in Rome, a seminary for American men preparing for the priesthood.

POPE JOHN PAUL II CELEBRATES MASS AT YANKEE STADIUM DURING HIS FIRST VISIT TO THE UNITED STATES IN 1979.

The long history between the Archdiocese and Yankees continued Oct. 2, 1979, when Pope John Paul II addressed 80,000 worshippers at Yankee Stadium. This time, he entered the stadium through the right field bullpen. The police were present in droves, with 2,000 along the motorcade and 1,000 inside the stadium.

In a slight contrast from Paul VI's messages about world peace, the emphasis of John Paul II's message at Yankee Stadium was on sharing.

And in keeping with that theme, John Paul II visited both of New York's baseball stadiums. He celebrated mass at Shea Stadium Oct. 3, where his words emphasized the unique qualities of New York City's urban pulse. He noted during that mass that New York was a city in need of finding a soul.

One man with an unusual connection to the first two papal visits to Yankee Stadium is Archbishop of Hartford Henry Mansell. In 1965, while a parish priest

— THE PAPAL VISITS —

for the Archdiocese of New York, Mansell provided live television commentary of the visit for New York station WPIX (for decades, the Yankees' flagship station).

In 1979, Mansell was directly responsible for the Vatican personnel who accompanied Pope John Paul II.

"I must say they were very good to work with," Mansell said from his office in Hartford, Conn., "Whenever the Holy Father is present, those experiences are unforgettable. Those experiences are a sign of the 'church universal,' and people of every racial and ethnic background come together.

"In 1979, the scene that caught so much of the world was the photos taken at Battery Park, at the tip of the island and with the Statue of Liberty in the background. That was where the Holy Father delivered an historic speech on human rights. We had arranged for that kind of setting in advance. Earlier that day there was a youth rally at Madison Square Garden, before we headed to Shea Stadium, and at the Garden they played the theme music from 'Rocky.' It just really connected with that young audience. And, of course, Yankee Stadium was an appropriate venue. Some would view it as a baseball cathedral."

As leaders in the Archdiocese of New York prepared for the 2008 visit by Pope Benedict VI, they were braced for logistical challenges.

"It is a tremendous amount of work, but it is very exciting," said Zwilling, the Archdiocese spokesman. "I was involved in 1995 with the last visit by John Paul II to New York. When you're getting ready for the visit, sometimes you get so wrapped up in the details you don't see the big picture.

"When you're actually there with the Pope and see the reaction of the people and know the tremendous impact the Pope is having on people – and how much it means

to people to be with the Pope and share mass with him, or even to see him as he goes by – it is just tremendously fulfilling and gratifying on both a professional and faith level."

Yankee Stadium's earliest documented history with a major, highly attended religious event extends back nearly six decades. A reported crowd of 87,195 was inside the stadium Aug. 6, 1950 for the international convention of the Jehovah's Witnesses.

> ## "THERE HAS BEEN NO PLACE IN OUR COUNTRY THAT HAS HOSTED MORE THAN ONE MASS WITH OUR HOLY FATHER, EXCEPT FOR YANKEE STADIUM."
>
> — JOSEPH ZWILLING —

There was such an overflowing collection of people, in fact, that the New York City Fire Department ordered other hopeful attendees outside the stadium. They heard the address via loud speakers.

The message delivered was rather stark.

"'Armageddon may come before another international convention of Jehovah's Witnesses can be held,' their leader predicted yesterday before a crowd of disciples that set a new high for attendance at Yankee Stadium," the *Times* reported.

Despite the large crowd for the event, the cleanup effort was quickly completed.

Roughly 500 people volunteered to report to Yankee Stadium for a daily 7 a.m. cleanup call. Within two hours, the bleachers and grandstands were clean and the flowers freshened near the second base sermon platform. Observers attributed the efficiency of the cleanup effort to the clean lifestyle of the Witnesses, who do not smoke and did not bring hot dogs, peanuts or other food items into the ballpark.

From those early origins we come to 2008, when the ambitious trip for Pope Benedict VI brought him not just to Yankee Stadium but also to the new ballpark for the Washington Nationals in Washington, D.C. □

A LONGTIME SPORTSWRITER FOR NEWSPAPERS AND THE WEB, MIKE LURIE IS CURRENTLY A SPORTS REPORTER ON WTOP RADIO AND WORKS IN INSTITUTIONAL ADVANCEMENT AT UMBC.

HOME SWEET HOME

Thanks for being home to 86 years of great baseball, from the home of everything you need while you're on the go.

 Mobil

Life. On the Run

It is an invitation-only affair, attended annually by an exclusive group of men with varying degrees of talent. Black tie is optional, but such an accessory would probably look foolish on a freshly pressed pinstripe suit.

Old-Timers' Day at Yankee Stadium is a tradition savored by both the participants and the fans. Once every summer, many of the finest players in the grand history of the New York Yankees franchise return to the Bronx to play a little baseball and do a whole lot of talking.

Joe DiMaggio, Mickey Mantle, Whitey Ford, Phil Rizzuto, Yogi Berra and Reggie Jackson are among those who have played on Old-Timers' Day at Yankee

Recalling the moment in his book "Ball Four: The Final Pitch," Bouton wrote, "I climbed out of the dugout and started for first base. I felt unsteady, like I might topple over. I heard a roar. 'What if I fell down?' I wondered. It seemed as if I was moving in slow motion, or underwater. At some point my hearing went out. I was moving in a white zone, watching myself slap hands with the other players. I took my place at the end of the line, numb, trying to figure out what had happened."

Then there was Casey Stengel, who boycotted the event for a decade after being fired as manager of the Yankees. He returned in 1970, during a time when the team held a party for the honored guests and their wives. Each player also received a gift, such as a clock

★ OLD-TIMERS' DAYS

BY: David Ginsburg

Stadium. Goose Gossage, a 2008 Hall of Fame inductee, has showcased his trademark mustache and wicked fastball in the game.

Greatness, however, is not a prerequisite for an invitation. Catcher Charlie Silvera spent much of his nine years with New York as the backup to Berra, who asked for a day off only a bit more frequently than Lou Gehrig. From 1948 through 1956, Silvera never played more than 58 games in a season. In 201 career games with the Yankees, he hit exactly one home run and finished with a grand total of 52 RBIs.

Yet Silvera has been a part of Old-Timers' Day far more often than Jim Bouton, who went 28 years without receiving a coveted invite because of the secrets he revealed in his tell-all book, "Ball Four."

Bouton's banishment ended after his son, Michael, wrote a letter to the New York Times on Father's Day 1998, asking the Yankees to allow the knuckleballer one more chance to don the pinstripes. Upon his return July 25 of that year, Bouton was so overcome by emotion he nearly fainted.

radio or a camera.

"He called the next day from California," Yankees public relations executive Marty Appel told the New York Times. "He didn't know who I was, but he said, 'Mrs. Stengel and I had a marvelous time. And thanks for the prize!'"

The first Old-Timers' Day at Yankee Stadium was held in 1947. It has since become one of the most coveted events on New York's home schedule, mostly because of the amazing assemblage of talent. But it also provides the fans and players a chance to revel in the past.

"Just being there with the legends – DiMaggio, Mantle, Yogi, [Bill] Dickey, Ford – was amazing," Silvera said. "Being a part of this franchise's great past, to see the guys, that's the big thrill."

The stats on Silvera's baseball card are hardly noteworthy; in fact, he still jokes about his longevity on a team that featured some of the greatest players in baseball history.

"I wasn't Casey Stengel's illegitimate son, but I did

— OLD-TIMERS' DAYS —

★

YOGI BERRA, WHITEY FORD, MICKEY MANTLE AND JOE DIMAGGIO TAKE PART IN OLD-TIMERS' DAY ON AUG. 3, 1974.

the job when called upon," he said. "When you play with all those Hall of Famers, you'd better perform to the best of your ability," he said.

Silvera played well enough to be part of six world championship teams, and he claims to be one of only eight players on the roster throughout a stretch in which New York won five straight American League pennants from 1949 to '53.

"It's a career that couldn't be scripted," the 83-year-old said. "I wasn't a star, but I was good enough to get invited back every now and then."

The same can be said of former Yankees infielder Phil Linz, who received more acclaim for playing the harmonica on the team bus than excelling on the field. But he is still a part of Yankees lore and darned proud of it.

Linz has been invited to participate in Old-Timers' Day about a dozen times. In 1980, his 5-year-old son posed for a picture with DiMaggio, and that photograph still stands in a prominent location in Linz's Connecticut home. He still recalls how DiMaggio hit a home run in that game, a liner down the left field line.

In later years, DiMaggio opted not to suit up because he figured it was better to be remembered for his play in his prime.

"Your biggest fear is embarrassing yourself," Linz said. "Almost everybody is thinking, 'I hope they don't hit the ball to me.' You don't want to field the ball, you don't want to throw it."

But Linz recalls one Old-Timers' Day in which he had to chase down a fly to short left field. From his shortstop position, Linz began pursuit on a rain-soaked field. He slipped into a slide, and the ball landed in his glove as the crowd roared its approval.

"They thought I did it on purpose, and I wasn't going to let anyone know otherwise," he said with a chuckle.

The game itself is secondary to simply showing off the varied collection of stars. The fans love seeing several generations of Yankees talent, and the players enjoy chatting with old friends and making new ones.

"You only play for around 20 minutes, depending on how long the introductions take," Linz said. "The best part is the camaraderie. They put you up Friday through Sunday, so you get to talk to some of your former teammates and bond with some guys you never played with. It's great."

The Yankees usually try to welcome at least one or two newcomers each year in order to provide a certain level of freshness to the event. As noted earlier, lofty career statistics are nice, but not a necessity. In 2006, when David Cone and Darryl Strawberry made their debut at Old-Timers' Day, they were joined by first-timers Steve Kemp (1983-84), Bobby Meacham (1983-88), Ross Moschitto (1965, 1967) and Dennis Rasmussen (1984-87).

Not exactly "Murderers' Row," but don't tell those guys they didn't belong there.

Last year, outfielder Paul O'Neill, a member of the Yankees from 1993 to 2001, played in his first Old-Timers' Day. He was only 44, a youngster compared to several of the other participants. Although he was

not far removed from a career in which he helped the Yankees win four World Series titles, O'Neill considered his return to the Bronx a thrilling trip down memory lane.

"You've got to be big around here to get an invitation," he said. "Let's face it, when you get out on this field, it brings back a lot of memories."

Even those who don't get onto the field have a great time. "They've got enough young players to play, so now the old guys just sit and watch, which is fine with me," Silvera said.

Other first-time participants at last year's game were Jesse Barfield (1989-92), Homer Bush (1997-98, 2004), Eli Grba (1959-60), Ken Griffey Sr. (1982-86) and George Zeber (1977-78). The event marked the 30th anniversary of the 1977 world champions. Of that team, 13 members were invited, including Jackson, Ron Guidry, Graig Nettles and Chris Chambliss.

The Old-Timers' Day now usually matches the Yankees against the Yankees, but in the past, New York summoned foes from the past. Former Boston Red Sox pitcher Tracy Stallard was brought in during an Old-Timers' Day event designed to honor the 1961 Yankees, who strolled to an AL pennant before dismissing the Cincinnati Reds in five games to win the World Series.

Stallard was with the Red Sox when he yielded Roger Maris' record-breaking 61st home run in the final game of the 1961 season.

"I've got a lot of memories, and sure, I'll never forget that," Stallard, now 70, said of Maris' drive into the right-field seats. "It doesn't bother me one

"YOUR BIGGEST FEAR IS EMBARRASSING YOURSELF. ALMOST EVERYBODY IS THINKING, 'I HOPE THEY DON'T HIT THE BALL TO ME.'"

— PHIL LINZ —

— OLD-TIMERS' DAYS —

bit. If not for that home run, a lot of things wouldn't have happened to me. It made me famous. I now go to card signings, and people always come up to me and talk about it."

It also earned him a one-time invite to Old-Timers' Day at Yankee Stadium. Stallard remembers retiring every batter he faced. "They hit groundballs and popped up," he said with pride. But his most treasured memory of the event was a conversation he had with Mantle in the New York dugout.

"We were good friends. We talked about the old times, people we knew, things we were doing after baseball," Stallard said. "Really, that's the best part about Old-Timers' Day. Seeing the guys, talking about the game and catching up with all the people you played with. Of course, being there makes you feel proud. The fans treated me good too, even though I never played with the Yankees."

This year's game will likely feature Gossage, scheduled to make a far more important trip to Cooperstown before stopping by for the final Old-Timers' Day at Yankee Stadium as we know it. Gossage may have plenty of gray in that droopy mustache, but he can still fit into his pinstripes quite nicely.

About that uniform. There was a time when the Yankees fit the old-timers for jerseys and pants before the game and took back the garb afterward. Now, each participant gets a uniform that he can take home as a keepsake.

"That's a nice little bonus," Silvera said.

Although he already has his share of uniforms in the closet, Silvera would like nothing more than to add another set of threads to the wardrobe he has assembled in his California home.

"They never did honor that 1953 team for winning a fifth straight pennant," Silvera said. "I'm hoping to get an invite this year because I want to see Yankee Stadium for the last time."

Linz feels the same way.

"I'm hoping to get invited because this is the last year of Yankee Stadium. I call and tell them I'm local, that it would be easy for me to come, but it's hard to get invited when you're not a premier player."

It has been three years since Linz has been asked to attend, but the 68-year-old hasn't abandoned hope of adding another layer to his fond memories of Old-Timers' Day. Silvera, perhaps, put it best.

"To go to New York and be recognized as a Yankee," he said, "well, there's nothing better." ☐

★

BILLY MARTIN, LEFTY GROVE AND PHIL RIZZUTO
SHARE A LAUGH BEFORE OLD-TIMERS' DAY.

DAVID GINSBURG HAS BEEN A SPORTSWRITER FOR THE ASSOCIATED PRESS SINCE 1983 AND SPORTS EDITOR OF THE BALTIMORE BUREAU FOR THE PAST 18 YEARS.

Baseball fans will say goodbye this year to Yankee Stadium – perhaps the most important sports home ever built in America. There will be commemorations, honors and memories shared about the hallowed baseball palace. The names of baseball gods like Babe Ruth, Lou Gehrig, Joe DiMaggio and Mickey Mantle will be invoked.

However, according to ballpark historians, the place where Ruth, Gehrig, DiMaggio and Mantle once roamed majestically isn't quite the same place that is hosting the Yankees' final season.

Yankee Stadium may be in the same location where it was when Colonel Jacob Ruppert bought the 10

had not won a pennant since 1964, the longest drought the club had experienced since the ballpark opened.

The ballpark reflected those hard times. It was difficult to maintain, and with state-of-the-art ballparks opening all around baseball in places like Pittsburgh, Cincinnati and St. Louis, along with the rise of the New York Mets, the Yankees needed a new home. Instead, though, a plan was drawn up to renovate the ballpark with New York City footing the bill, a controversial decision because of the economic woes of the city.

New York, like most American cities at the time, was in decline and on the brink of bankruptcy. Three years later when the city was bankrupt, one of the more famous tabloid headlines when New York asked

CONSTRUCTION ZONE

BY:
Thom Loverro

acres of land at the corner of Eighth Avenue and 155th Street for $600,000 more than 80 years ago. But two years of renovations in the mid-'70s turned it into a distinctly different ballpark than the one that opened with fanfare in 1923.

"The Yankee Stadium sitting there now is not the one that Babe Ruth played in, not the one Lou Gehrig played in," said Joe Mock, author of "Joe Mock's Ballpark Guide" and operator of www.baseballparks. com. "That was basically torn down in the 1970s and rebuilt with the renovations they did. Basically, it is a 1970s ballpark and not a 1920s ballpark like it was."

In 1974 and '75 much of the stadium was torn down and rebuilt. An entire generation of fans has grown up with this version of Yankee Stadium as its frame of reference. But historians see two different ballparks. "It was a very different stadium when it was renovated," said Philip Lowry, author of "Green Cathedrals."

By 1972, nearly 50 years after "the House that Ruth Built" opened, the franchise was not the dynasty that had ruled baseball for more than 40 years. The Yankees

for federal help was President Gerald Ford's response: "Ford to City: Drop Dead."

In 1972, Mayor John Lindsay came up with a plan for the city to buy the stadium for $24 million and then approved a plan to refurbish the stadium. The Yankees would play their home games at the Mets' ballpark, Shea Stadium, for the 1974 and 1975 seasons, and would return to Yankee Stadium April 11, 1976. More than 54,000 fans came out for the Yankees' return and an 11-4 win over the Minnesota Twins. Later that year, the Yankees returned to the World Series for the first time since 1964.

Fans saw a different ballpark when they came back. The stadium had the first instant replay screen in baseball. The 118 columns that had supported each tier of the grandstands were gone, as well as the distinctive frieze that had surrounded the top of the stadium. The seats were replaced with new, wider ones, and the upper deck was expanded upward. Many bleacher seats were cut out, and some were replaced with the black, unused area beyond center field.

— CONSTRUCTION ZONE —

A new middle tier section was constructed with an expanded press box and 16 luxury boxes. The capacity was now listed at 57,545.

Playing dimensions were changed as well. Left-center field was reduced to 430 feet, center field to 417, and right-center field to 385.

"It is two different ballparks," said former Yankees catcher Johnny Blanchard, who played at Yankee Stadium for eight seasons, retiring in 1965. "I understand business and why they did it, but I wish they had left it the way it was. I would say Mick would have had 10 more home runs. I saw him hit at least 10 balls to the warning track in left and right center. He would have rewritten the records for home runs. We hit 240 home runs as a team [in 1961] without a [designated hitter], and in this ballpark we would have hit 300 home runs."

Fans loved the comfort and amenities. But politically, it was a disaster, costing the city more than $100 million, and it became known in some circles as "the House that Lindsay Rebuilt." And the renovations may have taken away some of the best features of the ballpark.

★

"THE YANKEE STADIUM SITTING THERE NOW IS NOT THE ONE THAT BABE RUTH PLAYED IN, NOT THE ONE LOU GEHRIG PLAYED IN."

— JOE MOCK —

★

"I absolutely think pre-renovations it was a classic stadium," Lowry said. "You had that incredible white frieze that curved around the top of the ballpark, with vertical white columns, with an arch on the bottom. Then when they renovated the stadium in 1974 and 1975, and ready to play in 1976, instead of it being all around the stadium at the top of the third deck, they had it at the top of the bleachers in center and right field, and it didn't look right. It belonged where it had been since 1923, at the top of the third deck all the way around."

At the time though, there was very little sentiment for preserving old ballparks. No one was building retro ballparks like Camden Yards (which at $110 million in 1992, cost $50 million less than the Yankee Stadium refurbishing 16 years earlier). And the ballpark needed to be upgraded.

"It needed to be renovated," Mock said. "It would have been the same as old Comiskey Park in Chicago, and no one was happy with that place near the end of its life." □

THOM LOVERRO IS A COLUMNIST FOR THE WASHINGTON TIMES AND HAS PUBLISHED SEVERAL BOOKS, INCLUDING "HOME OF THE GAME: THE STORY OF CAMDEN YARDS."

★ YANKEE STADIUM DIMENSIONS (IN FEET)

1923	DISTANCE (DATES)	THROUGH 1973	1976	1985	1988 - 2008
LEFT FIELD FOUL POLE:					
281	281 (1923-27)	301	312	312	318
LEFT-CENTER FIELD:					
460	460 (1923-36)	457	430	411	399
CENTER FIELD:					
490	461 (1937-66)	463	417	410	408
RIGHT-CENTER FIELD:					
429	429 (1923-36)	407	385	385	385
RIGHT FIELD FOUL POLE:					
295	295 (1923-38)	296	310	310	314

I t's not a cemetery, but it looks like one, and it's understandable that young baseball fans walking through Yankee Stadium's Monument Park might think that all-time Yankees greats like Babe Ruth and Lou Gehrig are buried beneath the tombstone-like memorials and plaques awarded to a chosen few.

"Some are alive, and some are dead," said Yogi Berra, the oldest living member of the Yankees players and managers honored.

There are actually only five monuments in Monument Park, but 22 plaques also adorn the walls erected in the shrine located behind the left-center field fence between the Yankees' and visitors' bullpens. The five monuments all awarded posthumously were dedicated chronologically

six AL pennant winners and three World Series champions during the rise of the Yankees' first "dynasty." Huggins' 1,413 wins rank 21st on the all-time list, including a 1,067-719 record with the Yankees. He was inducted into the National Baseball Hall of Fame in 1964. Perhaps Huggins' greatest accomplishment was managing the almost unmanageable Ruth during the Bambino's first 10 years in New York.

★

JACOB RUPPERT

Gentleman–American–Sportsman. Through whose vision and courage this imposing edifice, destined to become the home of champions, was erected and dedicated to the American game of baseball.

The first of Monument Park's plaques was dedicated to former Yankees owner Jacob Ruppert and originally hung on the stadium's center field wall April 19, 1940. Ruppert

MONUMENT PARK
LEGENDS

BY:
Charlie Vascellaro

to Miller Huggins, Gehrig, Ruth, Mickey Mantle and Joe DiMaggio.

The plaques include numerous living and dead Yankee legends as well as one dedicated to Jackie Robinson in honor of the 60th anniversary of his arrival as the first black major leaguer. A pair of plaques also commemorates Catholic masses conducted by Pope Paul VI and Pope John Paul II and there is a monument dedicated to the victims and rescue workers of the attacks on New York City Sept. 11, 2001.

The following is a history of the placement of monuments and plaques in the original Yankee Stadium and the current Monument Park.

★

MILLER HUGGINS

As a tribute to a splendid character who made priceless contribution to baseball and on the field brought glory to the New York club of the American League.

Huggins was the first Yankee to be honored with a monument dedicated May 30, 1932 and placed within the field of play in front of the flagpole, which stood in center field at the original Yankee Stadium. Serving as Yankees manager for 12 seasons (1918-1929), Huggins presided over

inherited his father's Jacob Ruppert Knickerbocker Brewery and purchased the Yankees in 1915. He moved to begin construction on Yankee Stadium in 1921, purchasing a 10-acre lot in the Bronx from the estate of William Waldorf Astor across the river from where the Yankees had shared the Polo Grounds with the National League's New York Giants in Manhattan. The Giants, tired of being outdrawn by the Yankees and marquee attraction Ruth, had effectively evicted Ruppert's club, prompting the move. Giants skipper John "Muggsy" McGraw ridiculed the move, saying, "They're going up to Goatville, and before long they will be lost sight of."

★

HENRY LOUIS GEHRIG

A man. A gentleman and a great ball player whose amazing record of 2,130 consecutive games should stand for all time.

Gehrig was the first major league player to have his uniform number retired, an event which took place on Lou Gehrig Day at Yankee Stadium July 4, 1939, when the "Iron Horse" delivered his "luckiest man on the face of this earth" speech. Gehrig's monument was dedicated shortly after his

— MONUMENT PARK LEGENDS —

ORIGINALLY ON THE FIELD ITSELF, THE MONUMENTS TO LOU GEHRIG, MILLER HUGGINS AND BABE RUTH NOW STAND BEHIND THE CENTER FIELD FENCE.

death two years later and was the first such memorial to honor a Yankees player.

GEORGE HERMAN "BABE" RUTH

A great ball player, a great man, a great American.

As if there are words to describe Ruth's multitude of accomplishments and the immensity of his larger than life persona, the raised lettering on Ruth's monument makes a great attempt at summarizing the Babe's enormous life succinctly. Dedicated a year after his death April 19, 1949, the great Bambino's monument was placed to the right of Huggins' with Gehrig's on the left. Together, the three were approximately 450 feet from home plate, a long drive only occasionally reached by batters.

Writers Ira Berkow and Jim Kaplan described one such instance in their book on former Yankees manager Casey Stengel, "The Gospel According to Casey." "One day 'The Ol' Perfessor' was watching a center fielder struggle to track down a ball among the monuments, while the batter made his way around the bases. Stengel yelled out, 'Ruth, Gehrig, Huggins, somebody get that ball back to the infield!'"

ED BARROW

Barrow served as general manager under Ruppert, eventually rising to team president from 1939 to 1944

and chairman in 1945. Yankees squads assembled by Barrow captured 14 AL pennants and 10 Word Series championships during his 26-year tenure. Barrow's plaque was placed on the wall to the left of the flagpole April 15, 1954.

JOSEPH PAUL DIMAGGIO

"The Yankee Clipper"

DiMaggio's monument goes on to list his credentials as centerpiece of the great Yankees teams of the 1930s and '40s.

With a lifetime average of .325, DiMaggio won three MVP awards and two AL batting titles.

He hit in a record 56 consecutive games during the 1941 season.

Recognized as baseball's "Greatest Living Player"

MICKEY MANTLE

"A Great Teammate"

Mantle's monument is also a testament to his on-field accomplishments.

Mantle ended his career with 536 home runs and three MVP awards and was elected to the Hall of Fame in 1974.

Both DiMaggio's and Mantle's plaques were originally

— MONUMENT PARK LEGENDS —

dedicated June 8, 1969 on Mickey Mantle Day at Yankee Stadium. Mantle's plaque was handed to him by DiMaggio, and Mantle handed DiMaggio his plaque, saying, "His oughta be just a little bit higher than mine," and indeed it was hung just a little bit higher. The last two plaques to be placed on the field of play, they were moved to Monument Park after the 1974-75 renovations to the ballpark. Both were replaced by monuments shortly after Mantle's and DiMaggio's deaths.

★
JOE McCARTHY & CASEY STENGEL

The first new plaque added to Monument Park after the reopening of Yankee Stadium was dedicated to former manager Joe McCarthy April 29, 1976. Under McCarthy from 1931 to 1946, the Yankees won eight AL pennants and seven World Series, including four in a row from 1936 to 1939.

Three months later, July 30, 1976, the Yankees added a plaque for Stengel. Perhaps the greatest of all Yankees skippers, Stengel's squads won 10 AL flags and seven World Series during his 12 years at the helm, including a record five World Series in a row in his first five years as manager. Known for speaking in his own roundabout fashion, dubbed by New York baseball writers as "Stengelese," upon taking over the Yankees in 1949, Casey said, "There is less wrong with this team than any team I have ever managed."

★
THURMAN MUNSON

Yankees fans would have preferred that Thurman Munson's plaque not be added to Monument Park as early as it was, coming one year after his death in the crash of his jet. The first Yankee to be named team captain since Gehrig, Munson was a seven-time All-Star and three-time Gold Glove winner with a .292 career batting average in 10 big league seasons. Munson hit higher than .300 with more than 100 RBIs in three consecutive seasons from 1975 to 1977, becoming the first catcher to do so since Yankees Hall of Famer Bill Dickey, who accomplished the feat four times from 1936 to 1939. Munson's plaque was added to Monument Park Sept. 20, 1980.

★
ELSTON HOWARD

The plaque for another catcher, Elston Howard, was dedicated July 21, 1984. The Yankees' first black player, Howard also became the first black player to win the AL

Most Valuable Player award in 1963. A four-time All-Star, Howard played in 10 World Series with the Yankees during his 12 and a half seasons with the club and remained as a coach for the team from 1969 to 1980.

★
ROGER MARIS

Right fielder Roger Maris' plaque was placed in Monument Park July 21, 1984. Still best remembered for breaking Ruth's record of 60 home runs in a season, Maris hit 61 in 1961, but he also won back-to-back MVP awards in 1960 and 1961 and played on five consecutive pennant-winning Yankees clubs from 1960 to 1964, including two championship teams.

★
PHIL RIZZUTO

The Yankees retired Phil Rizzuto's No. 10 Aug. 4, 1985 and added another plaque to Monument Park. The ceremony included presenting Rizzuto with a cow adorned with a halo, in reference to the "Holy Cow" catch phrase he made popular as a Yankees broadcaster for 40 years. The cow proceeded to step on Rizzuto's foot and knock him over.

★
BILLY MARTIN

When asked for a rationalization of why Billy Martin deserved to have his No. 1 retired and a plaque dedicated in his honor Aug. 10, 1986, Yankees owner George Steinbrenner replied, "Being a Yankee has never meant more to anyone than it has to Billy Martin."

Martin added further justification. "I guess that some of the fans relate to me as a piece of every one of them, the guy in the street being aggressive fighting their boss," he said. "I fought for what I thought was right, and I couldn't worry about what City Hall thought." Martin served five separate stints as Yankees skipper (1975-78, 1979, 1983, 1985 and 1988).

★
LEFTY GOMEZ & WHITEY FORD

Lefty Gomez's and Whitey Ford's plaques were both dedicated Aug. 1, 1987. Gomez compiled a 189-102 record in 14 seasons, all with the Yankees, was a seven-time All-Star and pitched for the Yankees' four consecutive World Series-winning teams from 1936 to 1939. Gomez was elected to the Hall of Fame in 1972.

During his 16-year career with the Yankees, Ford

— MONUMENT PARK LEGENDS —

earned the nickname "Chairman of the Board" for his ability to remain calm in high-pressure situations. He compiled a franchise record 236 wins with 106 losses for a major league record .690 winning percentage among pitchers with at least 300 decisions. Ford pitched in 11 World Series with the Yankees and holds the records for World Series wins (10), losses (eight) and starts (22), as well as consecutive scoreless World Series innings pitched by a starter (33.2). Ford was named to 10 All-Star teams, won the 1961 Cy Young Award and was elected to the Hall of Fame in 1974.

★ BILL DICKEY

Dickey's 17-year career spanned from the end of the Ruth and Gehrig era through the great dynasty days of the DiMaggio and Rizzuto teams of the '30s and '40s until he was replaced behind the plate by Berra, who joined the Yankees in Dickey's final season. A lifetime .313 hitter, Dickey played for eight pennant winners and seven World Series champions and was elected to the Hall of Fame in 1954. A plaque honoring him was dedicated Aug. 21, 1988.

★ YOGI BERRA

Berra's plaque was placed in Monument Park in the same ceremony as Dickey's. At the end of his playing career, Berra held the record for home runs hit by a catcher, but he also played 260 games as an outfielder and recalls playing among the monuments in Yankee Stadium.

"It was all right," Berra said. "It was 461 feet, so there ain't too many going back there." Berra was elected to the Hall of Fame in 1972 and still holds records with 14 World Series appearances and 10 championships as well as World Series marks for games (75), at-bats (259), hits

(71), doubles (10), singles (49), games caught (63) and catcher putouts (457).

Now an automatic choice as one of the greatest baseball players of all time, Berra never gave a thought to being memorialized in Monument Park.

"Well you don't think about that when you're playing," he said. "Probably when you're finished, you wish you could be out there. It meant a lot; it felt good to get with all the great guys out there, Babe Ruth and Lou Gehrig. I walk through there once in while."

★

CATCHER THURMAN MUNSON PLAYED FOR THE YANKEES FROM 1969 TO 1979.

★ ALLIE REYNOLDS

Pitcher Allie Reynolds teamed with Berra on six World Series championship teams from 1947 to 1953. A five-time All-Star, Reynolds was honored with a plaque in Monument Park Aug. 27, 1989.

★ DON MATTINGLY

Perhaps the most popular Yankee in the early '80s, Don Mattingly was the Yankees' most consistent player during the second longest pennant and World Series drought in franchise history. He compiled 2,153 hits with a .307 lifetime average in 14 seasons. Mattingly's No. 23 was retired and his plaque was dedicated Aug. 31, 1997.

★ MEL ALLEN

"How about that?" wasn't so much a question as it was an exclamation that became the signature catch phrase for Mel Allen, who served two tremendous tours of duty (1939-1964, 1976-1989) as the Yankees' primary broadcaster on his way to becoming one of the first great voices of the game. He became the first non-player or executive to be honored with a plaque July 25, 1998.

— MONUMENT PARK LEGENDS —

★ BOB SHEPPARD

If Allen's was the voice of the Yankees to fans listening on the radio or television, Bob Sheppard's clear and concise diction has been an authoritative presence from above to the masses gathered at Yankee Stadium for more than half a century. Former Yankee Reggie Jackson dubbed him the "Voice of God." Sheppard called his first game in 1951, and when he was presented with his plaque May 7, 2000, he ended his acceptance speech with, "In April 2001, I intend to start my next 50 years in the booth. I see no reason for stopping." And he still hasn't.

★ REGGIE JACKSON

While Jackson may have spent most of his career in an Oakland A's uniform, it was as a Yankee that his "Mr. October" legend was secured, emphasized in the text of the plaque he received July 6, 2002:

"In five years in pinstripes, helped lead the Yankees to four division titles, three American League pennants and two World Championships.

At his best in October, belted four home runs on four consecutive swings in 1977 World Series — including three in Game Six at Yankee Stadium."

★ RON GUIDRY

In one of the most spectacular single-season performances by a pitcher, Ron Guidry solidified his place in Yankees lore by going 25-3, with an incredible league-leading 1.74 ERA, nine shutouts and 248 strikeouts in 273 innings. The man they called "Louisiana Lightning" racked up 170 wins in his 14-year career, all as a Yankee. Guidry's No. 49 was retired and his plaque presented Aug. 23, 2003.

DON MATTINGLY BATTED .307 DURING 14 SEASONS WITH THE YANKEES FROM 1982 TO 1995.

"I didn't expect any of that," he said. "They can always just say, 'OK, no one will have this number again.' But that monument ... that's not like a jersey. I've always been proud of what I did here. But I don't think I did anything to deserve what happened to me today."

★ RED RUFFING

Hall of Famer Red Ruffing anchored the pitching staff of the great Yankees dynasty teams of the 1930s and '40s, winning 20 or more games in four straight World Series championship seasons from 1936 to 1939. A six-time All-Star, Ruffing pitched for seven AL pennant winners and six World Series champions. He was elected to the Hall of Fame in 1967. Dedicated July 10, 2004, his is the last Yankees plaque to be placed in Monument Park.

★ JACKIE ROBINSON

The New York Yankees recognized the 60th anniversary of Robinson breaking baseball's color barrier with the last plaque added to Monument Park April 17, 2007. It contains the following inscription:

"In becoming the first Major League player to break the color barrier, Jackie will forever be an inspiration with his grace, dignity and perseverance. His story and the stories of those who never had the same opportunity must never be forgotten."

★

The success the Yankees have enjoyed during the past two decades has been fueled by a plethora of All-Stars and future Hall of Famers. And as the team prepares to move into a new stadium, fans will be eagerly awaiting the monumental moments to come. ☐

CHARLIE VASCELLARO IS A WRITER WHO SPECIALIZES IN BASEBALL AND BASEBALL HISTORY AND THE AUTHOR OF A BIOGRAPHY OF HANK AARON.

SOUNDS OF THE STADIUM

BY: Billy Altman

While any good baseball fan can tell you that nothing can match the excitement of watching a game in person at a major league park, doing so at Yankee Stadium is undoubtedly a unique and special experience.

From its striking outside architecture to the daunting Monument Park, Yankee Stadium has worn its long history proudly and often imposingly as well. But in between the pitches and the batted balls, in and around the on-the-field action, Yankee Stadium has also featured a variety of unique sounds (and sights) that in their own ways have been as emblematic to visitors as the familiar logo and pinstripes.

———————— ★ ————————

Bob Sheppard's unmistakable voice has been associated with the Yankees and Yankee Stadium for more than a half-century, and he delivers his announcements over the loudspeakers with such earnestness and authority that fans and players alike refer to him simply as "The Voice of God."

The career of the legendary Yankee Stadium public address announcer began in 1948 at Ebbets Field, when the then-Long Island high school speech teacher first handled PA duties for the football Brooklyn Dodgers of the old All-American Conference. Sheppard's cultured, deliberate style caught the ear of the Yankees football team,

FANS AND PLAYERS ALIKE REFER TO [PUBLIC ADDRESS ANNOUNCER BOB SHEPPARD] SIMPLY AS "THE VOICE OF GOD."

which hired him the next season when the Dodgers franchise folded and became part of the Yankees. The Yankees played their games at the stadium in the Bronx, and following the demise of the AAFC in 1950, baseball's Yankees immediately offered Sheppard their PA announcer's job.

The weekday demands of baseball conflicted with Sheppard's teaching work, though, and he at first declined. The Yankees persisted, and on Opening Day in April 1951, Sheppard announced his first Yankees starting lineup, which included Joe DiMaggio, Mickey Mantle, Yogi Berra and Phil Rizzuto.

The rest, as they say, is history. Sheppard's originally self-described "temporary job" has become a remarkable 57-plus-year tenure, 50 of which included PA duties for the football Giants as well.

In 2008, the native New Yorker remains the voice of Yankee Stadium, and suffice it to say that when he asks everyone to "please stand, and remove your caps" for the playing of the national anthem, you'd better believe none dare disobey the word of the good Sheppard.

———————— ————————

Sitting not far from Sheppard's press level perch for nearly four decades was another Yankees institution himself: Eddie Layton, whose mighty, 50,000-watt Hammond organ was a Yankee Stadium staple from 1967 until his retirement at the conclusion of the 2003 season.

It was the day that changed everything.

It began as a delightful September morning in New York, the sun bright and warm. Tuesday, a good day to get deep into the work week. The Yankees were on the road to another World Series. The Mets, having played in the World Series the previous October, were gamely trying to retain respectability.

It was a perfect day for flying.

Sept. 11, 2001.

The Yankees, after battering the Red Sox out of contention at Yankee Stadium, were enjoying a day off before flying to Chicago. The Mets had flown into Pittsburgh from Miami.

New Yorkers were on their way to work, newspapers folded in their special way for reading on the train. Some still at turned into horror.

The Mets were waking up in Pittsburgh. Mookie Wilson learned while surfing the Internet. Veteran Todd Zeile got a wakeup call from his wife in California. "For the first time in my lifetime I was losing the feeling of being safe," he said.

Tino Martinez of the Yankees was awakened in his Manhattan apartment by a phone call from his wife, Marie. He watched the Twin Towers crumble one after the other. "I was sick to my stomach," he said.

Millions of New Yorkers had personal experiences. I was 100 blocks uptown of the attack. Obviously there was no business for a sports columnist, so I became a news observer on the street. People rushed about, many asking where they could give blood. Veteran police detective Herb Griffin, stationed at Gracie Mansion, the mayor's

WE'RE ALL NEW YORKERS

BY: Steve Jacobson

home were awakened by the drone from the clock radio.

They heard the puzzled newscaster reporting a plane had just crashed into the North Tower of the World Trade Center, the tallest buildings on the New York skyline. Nothing more was known. It was 8:46 a.m.

News studios told of a military plane in 1945 that crashed in dense fog into the Empire State Building, then the tallest in the world. Today's sky was clear; this must have been a small plane staggering off course.

Minutes later, shocked broadcasters on the scene reported another plane had flown into the South Tower, a large airliner. It was deliberate, and the country was under attack. It was 9:03 a.m.

Those of a certain age dimly remembered hearing of the Japanese attack on Pearl Harbor that drew the country into World War II. People recalled Japanese kamikaze planes attacking military targets. These were suicide terrorists attacking civilians merely going to work. Americans were in a different kind of war.

Great clouds of smoke and fire billowed over that New York skyline. Emergency sirens screamed. The shock

official residence at 88th Street and the East River, was driving to work when he saw the collapse. "I've been shot at and pushed down stairs, and they were nothing," he said. "This, I was never so frightened in my life."

It was an awful day, and it was a day New Yorkers responded to memorably well.

Police and fire personnel who had good excuses to take off felt compelled by loyalty and turned around and went to work. One fire captain was supposed to be on a fishing boat off Long Island, but he heard the news and headed into the city. He paused on Southern State Parkway and wept for those already at the scene. Huge trucks with tons of sand were driven to block further attacks on hospitals, where stretchers lined sidewalks, and doctors and nurses awaited hordes of injured who never came. There were so few survivors.

The New York Fire Department suffered the loss of 341 firefighters. Police and other emergency services lost 62. The total of 2,603 dead in New York – 2,974 in the four hijackings – was larger than at Pearl Harbor; it was the worst toll of a single incident in American history.

Commissioner Bud Selig shut down baseball for a week.

— WE'RE ALL NEW YORKERS —

THE YANKEES LOGO RECEIVED A PATRIOTIC MAKEOVER FOR THE FIRST GAME AT YANKEE STADIUM AFTER SEPT. 11.

It was the first time baseball had called off all its games since D-Day in 1944. Some day fans would care again about the Yankees and Mets, but not now. The country was too filled with rage. A generation of young people who had never been gripped by war expressed collective anger they had not before shown. All people could be sure of was that they would be going to funerals and seeing strong men cry. So many rescue workers perished trying to save those in the towers. They rescued thousands.

The Mets bussed home from Pittsburgh because all commercial flights were grounded. From the New Jersey turnpike "we saw smoke coming from Ground Zero and no one could say anything," third baseman Edgardo Alfonzo said. "You could smell it. You could see the death of all the people. It was really quiet, and it made everyone cry."

For the first time in their professional lives, most of the athletes were vulnerable in their emotions and unshielded by their fame. They knew stockbrokers, investment bankers and friends who perished in the attacks. They knew that cars remaining in the dark of suburban commuter stations belonged to people lost in the towers.

At night New Yorkers didn't want to be alone in apartments

while the sirens wailed. People filled small restaurants and pubs late into the night, places where they could be close to other people. When a convoy of earthmovers and cranes, perhaps 40 yellow vehicles from upper Westchester County, rolled through the dark down Second Avenue, hundreds on the sidewalk stood and cheered.

The Yankees and Mets practiced that week at Yankee Stadium and Shea Stadium because that's what they do – and what else could they do? New York was beginning to fight back, and ballplayers were doing what they could do.

"For the first time I've seen, people here are not talking about baseball and the standings," Mets pitcher Rick White said.

Mets owners Fred Wilpon and Nelson Doubleday made cash contributions to the relief effort. Yankees owner George Steinbrenner made his donation. Mets players donated a day's pay each; the Yankees gave too, keeping the sums private.

Many players gave of themselves. The Shea Stadium parking lot became a staging point for relief supplies. Sweating and in workout shorts, manager Bobby Valentine helped organize relief workers and volunteers from his team as they hauled food, clothing and water onto trucks.

— WE'RE ALL NEW YORKERS —

Joe McEwing, a utility player, showed his range of skills by operating a forklift.

When the Yankees won their four championships during the Joe Torre era, they were celebrated by tickertape parades through what is known as the Canyon of Heroes. "Athletes are celebrated for what we do; we're definitely not heroes," Mike Piazza said. Instead, players celebrated firefighters and cops.

At Bellevue Hospital and the Hospital for Special Surgery some injured rescue workers rejected visits from dignitaries and welcomed the Mets as friends. "You visit those people, and maybe you made a difference for 20 minutes," Robin Ventura said.

"I thought it meant as much to me as it did to them," Zeile said.

Yankees visited hospitals and met cops and firemen on the smoldering pile of rubble. At the armory near Ground Zero, where rescue workers tried to catch their breath and people waited for word of loved ones, Bernie Williams approached a forlorn woman and told her, "You look like you could use a hug." Then he gave her one.

"All the people you meet ask for autographs," Derek Jeter said. "You feel you should ask them for their autographs."

So many people did what they could.

"I come from the South," Wilson said. "I had the impression that New York was distant and everyone was selfish. The more you're in New York, you find out New Yorkers are some of the most caring people in America."

"My generation has been a me-oriented society," Zeile said. "Maybe this is the crack in the 'Me Generation.'"

As America began to think about healing, baseball schedules were redrawn. The Mets' next series was shifted to Pittsburgh so the rescue operation could continue in the parking lots. The season was extended a week. Getting back to work was difficult, but New Yorkers were doing it.

Roger Clemens missed Yankees workouts to drive his wife and her friends back to Houston. One Yankee said it was good to get out of town. Jeter stayed home. "I couldn't turn the TV off," he said.

Baseball's role would be to turn lives back to some kind of normalcy. "People need an outlet," Wilson said. "It's also our outlet. I think we have an obligation." People still working on the site of destruction would have something to watch while they took a break.

Some people thought it was too soon for games when so many didn't have the benefit of closure. Baseball resumed Sept. 18. In New York, there was an emotional memorial ceremony at Yankee Stadium that embraced the city and more. It set a tone as only New York can. Bette Midler and tenor Placido Domingo sang. Mayor Rudy Giuliani lauded his city's response. At this time, New York was America's city, even the free world's city.

The Mets came home to New York, and when the Mets and Atlanta Braves came out to play at Shea Stadium, America came out with them.

"I'm so proud to be part of this, lucky to get people excited and yelling and smiling about this," said Braves manager Bobby Cox, who spent the best part of his brief playing career with the Yankees. That afternoon he kept to his New York routine of a long walk to the World Trade Center.

"WE'RE ALL NEW YORKERS."

— MIKE PIAZZA —

"It's so much worse than we could imagine," he said.

During the seventh inning stretch at Shea Stadium, Liza Minelli performed "New York, New York" with more than her customary exuberance, and the Braves loved it along with the Mets.

The electric drama came from the Mets, wearing caps reading, "FDNY," "NYPD" and "NYPA." Piazza, one of those who visited workers at the site more than once, came to bat in the last of the eighth inning with the Mets behind a run and a man on base.

"He's Casey," Zeile said. "Everybody on our bench thinks it's going to happen. How more fitting could it be? He swings, makes contact, and we know it's gone."

After the home run, Piazza didn't know if he should exult or not. "The sorrow and pain," he stammered. "If this helps ... we're all New Yorkers."

It was right and proper that the Yankees played in the World Series again; it belonged in New York. When the series turned from Arizona to New York for Game 3, that was apparent. A dozen players from the Diamondbacks,

— WE'RE ALL NEW YORKERS —

led by veteran first baseman Mark Grace, made their own unannounced pilgrimage to the vast hole that was Ground Zero.

"It was depressing," Grace said. "At the same time it was uplifting. Those people working 24/7 for eight weeks in the rubble. I needed to see it. Seeing it on TV, no way that happened; then you see the devastation."

He was experiencing what New Yorkers, Mets and Yankees had felt. "Anger, straight up," Grace said. "People did this for no reason. No reason."

The Arizona players were quickly recognized, and the group signed scraps of paper and posed for photos. One man wearing a Yankees cap went to Randy Johnson but turned his cap around first. "Maybe the rescue worker when he got home to his wife and children, instead of saying, 'We didn't find any bodies today,' his lead story was, 'Hey, Curt Schilling talked to us today, or Randy Johnson or Luis Gonzalez,'" Grace said. "No city could have handled this as well as New York."

The Diamondbacks may have felt admiration for New York, but Arizona led New York in the World Series, 2-0. For Game 3 at Yankee Stadium, security was heavy; President George W. Bush was coming.

Bush wore a sweatshirt emblazoned with "NYFD" in tribute to so many firefighters who gave so much and were still giving. He made a dozen practice throws under the grandstand. After all, he had been owner of the Texas Rangers and a sophisticated crowd of 57,000 would be watching.

Ceremonial tossers often make their pitch from well in front of the pitcher's mound. Jeter approached the president. "Better not throw from in front of the mound. They'll boo you," he cautioned. "Better not throw in the dirt. They'll boo you."

Properly warned, Bush went to the mound and gave a thumbs up. Then he made a good throw to backup catcher Todd Greene and walked off the mound to chants of "U-S-A, U-S-A!"

A tattered flag from the Twin Towers flew over the stadium. As "The Star-Spangled Banner" concluded, an American bald eagle was released from the bleachers and soared to a perch at the mound. A flight of freedom, it was called.

The crescendo was full. And the Yankees won the game. It was New York's moment as America's City. The Yankees won again in Game 4 and Game 5, too, sweeping the three games in New York, taking a 3-2 lead. It appeared destiny had taken hold.

Except that baseball knows no such empathy. The Diamondbacks, with their own motivations, won both games in Arizona and the championship.

New York would have no parade this time. Only pride and the continuing pain. New York endured. □

JOE TORRE DONNED A PORT AUTHORITY POLICE HAT FOR THE FIRST GAME BACK AT YANKEE STADIUM AFTER SEPT. 11.

STEVE JACOBSON WAS A COLUMNIST AT NEW YORK NEWSDAY FOR 25 YEARS AFTER 18 SEASONS AS A BASEBALL WRITER COVERING THE LORDLY YANKEES, THE ORIGINAL METS AND EVERYTHING IN BETWEEN. HE HAS COVERED OLYMPICS, SUPER BOWLS, FINAL FOURS, NBA, NHL, OLYMPIC GAMES AND FUN AND GAMES. HE WAS TWICE NOMINATED FOR THE PULITZER PRIZE. HIS LATEST BOOK IS "CARRYING JACKIE'S TORCH."

biggest beneficiaries. But this can't be something that goes on and on forever. Then perhaps we should move the game to Russia."

That deal set up a system in which 12 of the wealthiest teams in baseball paid into a pool that was divided up among 14 of the poorer teams, ensuring that virtually every team in baseball was included in the process at some point. After beating the Atlanta Braves in six games in the 1996 World Series, the Yankees (the largest contributors to the pool) were charged about $5.25 million. The Yankees were happy, the players were happy, and the public was happy; there would be no further labor interruptions until the new millennium.

But the owners weren't happy. Bolstered by a strong farm system, trades and some key free agent signings, the Yankees won the World Series again in 1998. And 1999. And 2000. All the while, they spent more and more on their payroll, unbothered by the relative pittance they were putting into the revenue-sharing pool because they were making far more than $5-10 million a year extra by winning the World Series.

Meanwhile, lower-paying teams floundered. Commissioner Bud Selig testified in front of a House of Representatives committee in 2001 that from 1995 through 1999, no team in the bottom half of the major leagues in payroll had won a postseason game. More changes were needed, changes that could allow low-budget teams the ability to compete, he said.

Following the 2002 season, the owners devised a new system that revised the luxury tax, lowering the percentage teams would pay into the pool, but raising the threshold that triggered it. After hammering out an agreement with the players' union, baseball's owners ratified the new revenue-sharing plan with a 29-1 vote.

Guess who dissented this time?

It was a deal that seemed aimed at reining in the Yankees as much as at helping teams in markets such as Pittsburgh, Kansas City and Montreal compete. Coming to that conclusion wasn't a big leap to make, given the atmosphere.

"I've been in the negotiating room several times," said relief pitcher and then-Yankees players' union representative Mike Stanton. "[Negotiators for the owners] have no qualms about not just saying 'big-market clubs' but saying 'the Yankees.' Everyone hates the Yankees until the Yankees come into town and play in front of 50,000 people."

The end result? From 2003 through 2007, only three major league teams had to pay the luxury tax – the Yankees ($121.6 million), the Red Sox ($13.9 million) and the Angels ($927,059).

The Yankees and their exorbitant payrolls were dominating the system and helping support a few small-market teams that couldn't or wouldn't support themselves. But the luxury tax proved an unlikely saving grace in the movement for a new Yankee Stadium thanks to one giant loophole: Teams could deduct parts of their stadium maintenance and construction costs from their luxury tax hit.

In other words, a team could either pay to build its own stadium, or it could pay the other major league teams that made less money.

For Steinbrenner, financing the stadium suddenly became an economical decision. They could continue to demand the city and state foot part of the bill and possibly not get the new park, or they could cover the cost privately and stop paying the other major league teams to compete with them. It was a win-win decision and possibly a big-time moneymaker in the long run. Without the Yankees' money, perhaps those other teams wouldn't be able to afford to pay as many multimillion-dollar contracts, perhaps affecting their play on the field. Maybe it would give the Yankees a better shot at winning a World Series, generating even more revenue for the team. Meanwhile, the new stadium would bring in money too – and even more if it was owned and financed completely by the

"WE TRIED TO REFLECT A FIVE-STAR HOTEL AND PUT A BALLFIELD IN THE MIDDLE."

— LONN TROST —

— THE YANKEES' NEXT HOME —

team, with no provisions to split income.

It was a way for Steinbrenner to flip those other 29 owners the bird, a way for him to win the luxury tax battle in the long run.

And everybody knows how much Steinbrenner likes to win.

★

Just over a year before the new stadium's scheduled opening, the Yankees officially renamed their spring training facility and minor league complex in Tampa, Fla., George M. Steinbrenner Field. But the new Yankee Stadium is the one with the finger-prints of the Steinbrenner family all over it.

The Steinbrenner family, George, along with sons Hank and Hal and former son-in-law Steve Swindal, wanted a Yankee Stadium that paid homage to the franchise's history while still bringing the facilities and amenities into the 21st century. As chief operating officer Lonn Trost said while hosting a tour of the still-in-progress new $1.3 billion stadium, "We tried to reflect a five-star hotel and put a ballfield in the middle."

That meant including a conference center for use by corporate meetings by day and a great view of the game at night. It also meant an on-site concierge whose job it will be to secure reservations at restaurants or tickets to theater shows for some ticketholders. The plans include more luxury suites, a massive video screen, a martini bar and new party suites — not to mention wide concourses, more restroom facilities and more concessionaires. A five-star hotel, indeed.

While there are many improvements that will

GEORGE STEINBRENNER AND THE YANKEES BROKE GROUND FOR THE TEAM'S NEW STADIUM ON AUG. 16, 2006.

benefit the average fan, the most impressive facets of the new stadium are what it can offer the Yankees' increasingly wealthy clientele. The plans included a decrease in stadium capacity (from 56,886 to 52,325 including standing room), meaning fewer upper deck seats (down from 28,300 to about 17,000) but more lower deck seats (from 25,300 to about 32,000). At the same time, the upper deck will be moved back from the field a few feet with a more gentle slope to the top of the stadium, meaning that fans in the top few rows will be about as far from home plate in the new stadium as the old one. Around the stadium will be a new Metro North train station to allow fans easier access to the stadium and reduce pregame and postgame traffic, as well as several new parking decks.

On the field, meanwhile, there are few major changes planned. The field dimensions are scheduled to remain the same (318 feet down the left field line, 399 to the deepest part of left-center, 408 to center, 385 to the deepest part of right-center and 314 down the right field line) as they have been since 1988, the last time the Yankees moved the fences. The amount of foul territory is planned to be about the same as the old stadium.

The game will look mostly the same. And as long as the Yankees keep winning, the background will look remarkably similar – with the stadium filled to the brim with fans.

Just as Steinbrenner wanted it. □

DAVID SANDORA IS A COPY EDITOR AT THE PITTSBURGH TRIBUNE-REVIEW AND WAS FORMERLY THE SPORTS EDITOR FOR METRO NEW YORK.

— THE TIMELINE —

Eddie Layton makes his Yankee Stadium debut.

May 14: Mantle hits his 500th career home run off Baltimore's Stu Miller.

1968

Sept. 25: In his final game at Yankee Stadium, Mantle gets the Yankees' only hit in a 3-0 loss to the Cleveland Indians.

1969

June 8: The Yankees host "Mickey Mantle Day" and retire his No. 7.

Oct. 11: Notre Dame routs Army, 45-0, in the 22nd and final meeting of the series at Yankee Stadium.

1971

May 5: The New York Cosmos of the North American Soccer League begin their first season with a 1-0 victory over the Washington Darts.

1972

Jan. 27: The Yankees sign an agreement with the Mets to share Shea Stadium in 1974-75 while Yankee Stadium undergoes renovations.

1973

Sept. 23: The New York Giants tie the Philadelphia Eagles, 23-23, in their final game at Yankee Stadium.

Sept. 30: The Yankees lose to the Detroit Tigers, 8-5, in the last game at the old stadium.

1976

April 15: The Yankees beat Minnesota, 11-4, in the opening of the remodeled Yankee Stadium. Twins outfielder Dan Ford hits the first home run in the new stadium.

Sept. 28: In the last championship fight at the stadium, Muhammad Ali beats Ken Norton in the 15th round in their third fight.

Oct. 14: Chris Chambliss hits a leadoff home run in the ninth inning to beat Kansas City, 7-6, in Game 5 of the AL Championship Series, sending the Yankees to the World Series.

1977

July 19: The National League wins the first All-Star Game in the renovated Yankee Stadium, 7-5.

Oct. 18: Reggie Jackson hits three home runs in three consecutive at-bats, all on the first pitch, as the Yankees beat Los Angeles, 8-4, to win the World Series.

1978

June 17: Ron Guidry strikes out 18 Angels, in a 4-0 win, an AL record for a lefty.

1979

Oct. 2: Pope John Paul II holds mass.

1983

July 4: Dave Righetti throws a no-hitter against the Boston Red Sox as the Yankees win, 4-0.

July 24: Kansas City's George Brett loses a home run in the "pine tar game." The Royals' protest is upheld, the home run is allowed, and the game is completed Aug. 18.

1990

June 21: Nelson Mandela is welcomed.

June 22: Billy Joel performs in the first rock concert at Yankee Stadium.

1996

May 14: Dwight Gooden throws a no-hitter against the Seattle Mariners as the Yankees win, 2-0.

Oct. 26: The Yankees win their first of four World Series under manager Joe Torre with a 3-2 win over Atlanta in Game 6.

1997

June 16: The Mets' Dave Mlicki shuts out the Yankees, 6-0, in the first interleague game.

1998

April 15: A fallen expansion joint in the upper deck at Yankee Stadium forces the team to play at Shea Stadium. The Yankees beat the Angels, 6-3, and later that day, the Mets beat the Cubs, 2-1.

May 17: David Wells throws a perfect game against the Minnesota Twins as the Yankees win, 4-0.

— THE TIMELINE —

★

YOGI BERRA CONGRATULATES ROGER MARIS AFTER HIS RECORD-SETTING 61ST HOME RUN ON OCT. 1, 1961.

1999

July 18: David Cone throws a perfect game against the Montreal Expos as the Yankees win, 6-0.

2000

July 8: A rainout forces the Yankees and Mets to play a day-night doubleheader, with the first game at Shea Stadium and the second game at Yankee Stadium.

Oct. 22: Roger Clemens throws a broken bat barrel at the Mets' Mike Piazza in Game 2 of the World Series. Clemens had beaned Piazza July 8.

2001

Oct. 31: Derek Jeter's 10th-inning home run gives the Yankees a 4-3 victory to even the World Series with Arizona at two games apiece. Tino Martinez sends the game into extra innings with a two-run home run in the ninth. The next night, Scott Brosius forces extra innings with another two-run home run in the ninth. The Yankees lose the World Series in seven games.

2003

Oct. 16: Aaron Boone sends the Yankees to the World Series with an 11th-inning home run off Boston's Tim Wakefield to win Game 7 of the ALCS, 6-5.

Oct. 25: The Florida Marlins win Game 6, 2-0, in what was possibly the last World Series game at Yankee Stadium.

2008

July 15: Yankee Stadium hosts the 79th MLB All-Star Game.

Sept. 21: The Yankees are scheduled to play the Baltimore Orioles in the final regular season game at Yankee Stadium.

JOHN DELCOS COVERED THE NEW YORK YANKEES FROM 1998 TO 2005 FOR GANNETT NEWSPAPERS (THE JOURNAL NEWS) IN WESTCHESTER, N.Y. HE CURRENTLY COVERS THE NEW YORK METS AND MAJOR LEAGUE BASEBALL.

BY THE NUMBERS

YANKEE STADIUM ATTENDANCE RECORDS

> **SEASON**
> 2007 _____ **4,271,083**

> **SINGLE GAME, NIGHT**
> VS. BOSTON, MAY 26, 1947 _____ **74, 747**

> **SINGLE GAME, DAY**
> VS. BOSTON, SEPT. 26, 1948 _____ **69, 755**

> **DOUBLEHEADER**
> VS. BOSTON, MAY 30, 1938 _____ **81, 841**

> **SINGLE GAME AT REMODELED STADIUM**
> VS. OAKLAND, APRIL 10, 1998 _____ **56,717**

YANKEE STADIUM FIRSTS

> **GAME:** APRIL 18, 1923 (4-1 WIN OVER BOSTON)

> **BATTER:** BOSTON'S CHICK FEWSTER

> **YANKEES BATTER:** WHITEY WITT

> **HIT:** BOSTON'S GEORGE BURNS (SINGLE IN SECOND)

> **YANKEES HIT:** AARON WARD (SINGLE IN THIRD)

> **HOME RUN:** BABE RUTH (THREE-RUN HOMER IN THIRD)

★

BABE RUTH AND LOU GEHRIG ANCHORED THE YANKEES' "MURDERERS' ROW" LINEUP FOR MANAGER MILLER HUGGINS IN 1927, A TEAM MANY BELIEVE WAS THE GREATEST IN BASEBALL HISTORY.